Large-Leaved
Perennials

Large-Leaved Perennials

Myles Challis

WARD LOCK

First published in Great Britain in 1992
by Ward Lock Limited, Villiers House, 41/47 Strand,
London WC2N 5JE, England
A Cassell Imprint

Jacket Design by Jerry Goldie

Text filmset by Chapterhouse, The Cloisters, Formby

Printed and bound in Spain by Graficas Reunidas, Madrid

British Library Cataloguing in Publication Data. A catalogue
record for this book is available from the British Library.

Challis, Myles
  Large-leaved perennials. – (Foliage plant series)
  I. Title   II. Series
  635.932

ISBN 0 7063 7058 9

**Frontispiece: *Gunnera manicata*, the largest
leaved hardy perennial of all for majestic foliage
by the pool or lakeside.**

Contents

Preface

It has long been realized and brought to our attention by some of the great plants people and gardeners of our time, that a beautiful, well designed and most importantly *interesting* garden requires a foundation of attractive foliage, to complement the flowers and retain interest throughout the year.

A garden, regardless of its size, can be greatly enhanced if large-leaved perennials are incorporated into that foliage framework along with smaller or finer-leaved subjects. By including some of these plants, greater variety and therefore interest is created, as they increase the range of form, texture and even colour.

The aim of this book is to reveal the great value of large-leaved perennials in the garden and to show the sometimes spectacular results that can be achieved with them.

Large-leaved perennials possess many qualities which no garden should be without, indeed one could argue that a totally successful garden cannot be created without them. Many are architectural in form and therefore useful in bringing focus to a particular area of the garden, and are unbeatable for softening the hard lines of brick or concrete.

They create a lush, almost tropical atmosphere in a garden and will add great beauty to a pond or streamside where they are most at home.

Even the tiniest of backyards can accommodate a few of these plants, where even if they are grown in pots they will do much to improve the overall picture.

Large-leaved perennials are versatile plants and are generally very easy to grow, are more inclined to flourish than fade away unless thoroughly neglected, and their great variety of form adds a new dimension, giving contrast to the more general garden flora.

Every garden has its own individual character, but that character will be enhanced and become more striking and beautiful if the garden plays host to some of these large-leaved plants.

M.C.

This *Lysichiton*, the hybrid between the yellow *L. americanum* and the white *L. camtschatcensis*, is larger than both, and is as yet unnamed.

CHAPTER 1

Introducing large-leaved perennials

Big leaves are in – or, at least, becoming more widely appreciated! As with all things, fashions change and different styles and tastes evolve, and gardening and plants are no exception.

Who among us on seeing for the first time the great towering, spreading leaves of *Gunnera manicata* under which we could stand to shelter from the rain, could not fail to be impressed? Not many plants it is true, especially perennials, are built on such a Brobdignagian scale, but nevertheless there is a wealth of large and handsome leaves of every shape and form imaginable to be found among herbaceous plants. No one of course would want to fill their garden with gunneras, but one or two strategically placed in the right setting, preferably by a pond or lake, would be a showstopper. Some people have a fixed idea that only large gardens can accommodate large-leaved plants but, as we shall see, large leaves can act as an effective contrast to smaller-leaved specimens and actually enhance the design of a small garden. But for many gardeners, the boldness of large-leaved plants is something of an acquired taste.

There are, of course, exceptions to every rule and surely this must apply to hostas, appreciated probably by almost every gardener. Indeed, I am hazarding a guess here, but the popularity of hostas may have played an important role in the increasing interest in the use of foliage, if not large leaves in particular. They are first-class plants which no garden should be without. Hostas have become so popular that specialist societies have been formed in many countries and hosta breeders, especially in the USA, appear to have gone berserk, and consequently the number of varieties available nowadays is enormous. This being so, the genus has a book of its own in this series and only the largest-leaved varieties are dealt with in this book.

The aim of this book is to introduce the merits and advantages, and not least the beauty, of large-leaved perennials, and their potential and value in the garden. I am not suggesting, of course, that you should fill your garden with them, but by careful selection and positioning of some of them, great interest and beauty will undoubtedly be added to your garden.

Large leaves are an essential part of the garden scene, and a satisfactory one cannot be completed without them. They not only emphasize the smaller leaves, but are an important contrast (especially those of rounded outline) to the vertical shapes of plants such as grasses or the lacyness of ferns.

Garden styles, like the plants in them, wax and wane in popularity. I am myself a great advocate of the informal garden, because I feel that gentle curves rather than straight lines and geometric shapes best accommodate the natural forms of plants. However, formal gardens are certainly enjoying a resurgence in popularity, and leaves, especially large ones, are invaluable in helping to soften the harshness of angular paving or brickwork. International flower shows often make extensive use of paving in the garden exhibits and then give inspiration in the use of bold plantings to soften contours.

In informal gardens the generous shapes of large-leaved plants emphasize the rounded curves of beds and the more architectural forms provide a focus in the way a statue or sundial might in a more formal setting.

While speaking of 'points of focus' and 'style', why shouldn't the same principles of interior design be applied to gardening? Plants are as important in the garden as furniture is in the house, and their positioning, relation to one another, background etc., can equate to furniture, curtains, carpets and wallpaper. Plants can be used to create atmosphere in the garden just as effectively as any interior designer's materials in the house and it is perhaps here that the large leaves play an especially important role, as they so often possess 'architectural' qualities.

There will always be those who crave a rainbow of colour in the garden, but the restful qualities and more subtle tints of foliage do, I feel, give much more lasting pleasure. The gardener who concentrates on foliage in his or her garden for interest, and indeed colour, will be rewarded and satisfied far more than the individual who relies on short-lived annuals, for the period of interest which foliage gives is far greater – a particularly important factor to consider in the case of those who have smaller gardens.

The selection available is a varied one, as large leaves come in many forms, from the solid simple round shapes of hostas, ligularias or peltiphyllum to the much divided and toothed leaves of aruncus or melianthus, or the sword-like blades of phormium. Why nature has produced this profusion of shapes is difficult to answer, as plants, just like animals, birds or insects, have evolved over millions of years. We can, however, be fairly certain why some have larger leaves than others. The leaf, after all, is what enables a plant to function, given light, soil and water. Different plants have evolved to adapt to different conditions and, where water is concerned, the larger the leaf the greater the degree of transpiration because of the larger surface area. Thus, one way in which plants have developed to suit their environment is to produce large leaves where they can afford to lose moisture and small ones where they have to conserve it. Gunneras and lysichitons, for example, will thrive best in boggy conditions where there is a constant supply of moisture at the root; on the other hand, plants found growing in arid areas where little moisture is available usually have much smaller leaves.

If you look at the vegetation across the globe, it is very evident that the concentrations of plants with large leaves are not only to be found in the warmer regions, but also in areas of high rainfall such as the tropical forests. By studying the leaves of a gunnera or a banana, for example, you will see how the rain collected is directed to their centre to land on the soil where the main concentrations of root are.

As well as the hardy large-leaved perennials, I have selected a few tender ones. These have been included both for their great beauty and especially for their value in creating an atmosphere of tropical climes, as discussed in Chapter 5.

Perhaps, like me, you will catch the 'big leaf bug', something which can lead to extraordinary results. A visitor to my garden once remarked: 'you feel as Alice must have done when she ate the piece of mushroom which the Caterpillar gave her to reduce her size. Huge and wonderful leaves are above and all around you.'

I caught the 'big leaf bug' at the tender age of seven when I was taken for the very first time to Kew Gardens. Stepping into the Aroid House I was engulfed and enveloped by a jungle of gigantic leaves of every shape and form: I was mesmerized by it all, and hooked from that moment on.

9

CHAPTER 2

The value of architectural plants in the garden

Nature is amazing for her apparently limitless scope in producing variety of form both in the animal and plant worlds. She is the greatest designer that ever was, and ever will be, and much inspiration has been sought from her creations from time immemorial.

I cannot help but be reminded, when I stand under the vast leaf of a gunnera, of the vaulting of some great cathedral. Look at the segmented canes of a colony of giant bamboo and you have the strength and structure of stone buttressing.

The Greeks and the Egyptians decorated their buildings with the strong architectural forms of acanthus leaves, and plants such as the lotus were deemed sacred by them. In more recent times Art Nouveau drew complete inspiration from form of leaf and flower.

In the garden the value of plants with strong architectural shapes cannot be underestimated, particularly where modern hard landscaping has produced severe straight lines and geometric shapes. These can be broken or at least softened by natural plant forms, and this is most easily achieved with large-leaved subjects or groupings of plants with strong leaf character.

Here the fineness of the ivory, feathery plumes of *Aruncus sylvester* (*A. dioicus*) are set off by the huge leaves of *Gunnera manicata*.

Softening a hard landscape

The materials used in many modern buildings have a harshness which can be unattractive on its own. A modern house is often best complemented by a contemporary garden design, but a garden, after all, is not like an office or waiting room – it should possess an atmosphere which is conducive to relaxation and entertaining. The necessity, therefore, to use plants with architectural yet softening qualities is much greater in the case of modern, hard-landscaped gardens than with those of a more informal or 'natural' design, where their value is more for contrast in size, texture, colour and so on.

The greater the evidence of hard landscaping the larger the number of architectural plants will be required to obtain a satisfactory picture. This presents no problem as there is such a wealth and range of material to choose from, and naturally the greater the variety incorporated into the planting the better, and evergreens such as phormiums, play an important role here.

Phormium tenax, the New Zealand flax, consists of a great tuft of stiff, sword-like leaves standing 2 m (6 ft) high which are topped (in good summers) by even taller flower spikes which are equally architectural though not very colourful. This is an invaluable plant for instant effect, a landscaper's favourite.

Large plants such as phormiums should not be confined to large gardens. If they are combined with smaller-leaved plants in a small garden they will not

11

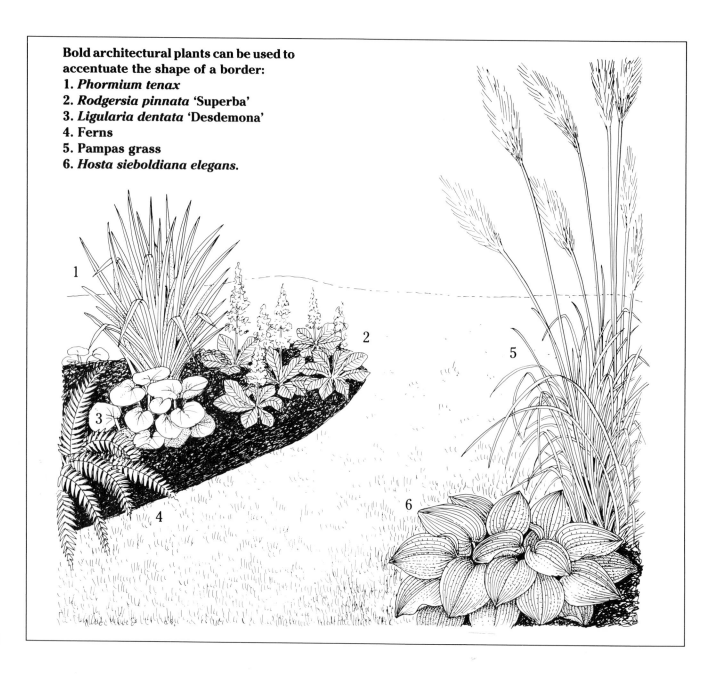

Bold architectural plants can be used to accentuate the shape of a border:
1. *Phormium tenax*
2. *Rodgersia pinnata* 'Superba'
3. *Ligularia dentata* 'Desdemona'
4. Ferns
5. Pampas grass
6. *Hosta sieboldiana elegans.*

only be of value for contrast in size and variation of shape, but give an illusion of size to the garden. Small plants on their own will do nothing to make a small garden seem bigger; equally a collection of purely large or large-leaved ones, no matter how varied, beautiful or architectural, will not be as effective as where they are combined with smaller or more delicately leaved plants. Where space is limited it is better to have fewer different plants, rather than to reduce too much the size of each individual clump, as then the character, and to a certain extent the beauty, of the plants is lost.

Providing emphasis

One of the greatest values of plants with strong architectural shapes is their use in emphasizing the design of the garden itself. Trees and shrubs obviously also play an important role here as they form the 'bones' of the garden, but bold architectural plants also give it structure.

Even in ordinary gardens regardless of their size architectural plants are of value. The eye is naturally drawn to them and because of this gives emphasis or draws attention to an area or feature. For example, steps can be marked or accentuated, or the location of a little bridge over a stream would be much more evident if architectural plants were situated by it.

If a large border swings out into the lawn to give shape to the garden, then this purpose is achieved more satisfactorily if this area of the border contains bold plants, which will give strength to the shape. This is particularly important where distance is concerned. Plants with strong, clearly defined shapes can be distinguished and appreciated from afar, whereas those with small or finely cut foliage must be observed close to. This variation of leaf size creates contrast and

therefore interest, the small leaves accentuating and complementing the large and vice-versa. The larger the garden the greater the necessity for use of plants of strong character, to add variation if nothing else.

Considering texture and colour

Variety is what creates interest and this is achieved also with contrast of shape, texture and colour.

First, colour. Certain colours do not harmonize, but nevertheless colours which people would not dream of putting together in a room or even with their clothes, are often used side by side in the garden. Similarly, where only two or three colours may be considered sufficient in a room, all hell is let loose in the garden, as a kind of colour blindness seems to take over. Some beautiful effects can be created with colourful planting, but gardens which rely on their beauty solely through the use of flower colour cannot ever be as successful as those where greater emphasis is put on plant character and leaf shape.

We do not have to omit colour by any means to achieve this, as even foliage comes in many shades – purples, pinks, yellows, reds, white as well as the many tints of green itself. Many plants with bold architectural leaves also possess beautiful flowers. Take the acanthus, for example. Apart from having the most sculptural leaves, it also possesses dramatic flower spikes of purple and white which are themselves an architectural feature of the plant. But if a plant does not have attractive foliage as well as flowers, then when the flowers have finished there is nothing worthwhile left to look at. The leaf is around usually far longer than the flower and is really therefore of greater importance.

It is leaf shape and size that basically gives large-leaved perennials their architectural qualities and we

13

should create as many contrasts with them as space allows. What could be more contrasting than, say, the spikiness of a yucca or phormium with the roundness and smoothness of a hosta, or the huge solidness of a gunnera leaf next to the much divided one of a heracleum or an aruncus. The round, scalloped leaves of peltiphyllum would be perfectly set off by the spears of a bog iris, while the serrated leaves of melianthus contrast well with those of the banana-like leaves of the canna.

Texture, too, adds another dimension of interest. At one extreme we have the acanthus with its highly glossy leaves, at the other the verbascum with its very woolly ones, and there are a whole host of variations in between. The leaves of ligularias are often described as oily smooth, and those of gunnera as puckered. Those of blue hostas can be glaucous and a rheum is matt. So in addition to the wide variety of leaf shape, we also have colour and texture increasing still further the value of these plants in the garden.

A tropical atmosphere

The Victorians realized at a very early stage the merits of these large-leaved plants. One can understand their enthusiasm when one realizes that many of the plants were new to them, having been recently introduced, but nevertheless they certainly appreciated their potential. Writers of the time, especially William Robinson, greatly influenced the style of gardening and the use of the new plants that the Victorians grew both in their gardens and their conservatories and greenhouses. The fashion of 'sub-tropical' gardening, which was a new and highly fashionable occupation of the time, was largely his innovation, and although it involved the use of a lot of greenhouse plants and hardy exotics such as bamboos, phormiums and so on, it also incorporated many large-leaved perennials because of their great usefulness in creating a tropical atmosphere.

Palms, cordylines and yuccas might be under-planted with acanthus, while an Abyssinian banana (*Ensete ventricosum*) might be given a fringe of hostas. The same style was used in the public parks of the time. Sometimes, both in private and public gardens, plants would be used on their own as lawn specimens. This is a very attractive way of displaying a highly architectural plant where the space is available. Plants which require as much sun as is available would obviously benefit from this kind of position.

Treated as specimens, the full individuality and character is best appreciated with large subjects such as bamboos or pampas grass, the giant reed, *Arundo donax*, or *Aralia cachemirica*, which, although a perennial, is 2m (6ft) high.

Tender bedding plants such as cannas are effective in bold clumps, and if the beds are raised they will do even better as the sun's heat is retained longer than in the surrounding level ground. Plants of lesser stature can provide a similar effect if planted in a bold group; as a lone specimen their character would be lost.

The potential of architectural plants is only realized when one has used them. What you have never had you do not miss, but try them and you will be enlightened!

Phormium tenax 'Variegatum', one of the most architectural of plants, good for creating exotic effects.

Large-leaved perennials can be used to 'accent' a spot. Here rheums (along with pampas grass) are used as sentinels to accent a bridge.

CHAPTER 3

Companion planting

The exact arrangement of the plants in a garden may not seem vital to the inexperienced, but the precise position of a tree, shrub, climber and even an herbaceous plant can contribute as much to the final effect as the positioning of furniture, pictures and ornaments can in a room. And, like planning a room, a well-thought-out colour scheme can make a world of difference in the garden.

.The 'art' of landscaping and planting demands even greater skill than that of the interior decorator, as he or she has to possess a combination of talents: that of horticulturalist and draughtsperson with an artist's eye for perspective and colour sense, married with imagination and vision. And so unless you are employing the skills of such an expert, it will necessitate much thought before planting, whether dealing with a virgin site or one already partially planted.

What follows can only be guidelines as every garden is different and should, indeed, be individual. Nevertheless much experience lies behind these suggestions, which I hope will save time and unnecessary mistakes, and although an entire garden cannot be planned by them the suggested companions and groupings should be of considerable help.

By creating contrast, by using plants of different sizes, forms, colours and textures, we achieve variety and therefore interest and, with the exception of colour, we need put no limits on these things. Because we are considering here companions specifically for large-leaved perennials I have excluded certain groups such as conifers, heathers, alpines, annuals and the cottage garden-type flowering plants. This is partly for aesthetic reasons and also simply because this book would need to be a good deal larger to include them. Companions for bog and waterside perennials are covered in Chapter 4, and the more tender plants such as banana, ginger, cannas and so on I have reserved for Chapter 5, because it is the sub-tropical style of garden to which they are best suited.

Deciding on a colour scheme

I consider the choice of colour the first decision to make when planning an area of the garden. A small area should be thought of as one 'room' and therefore have one colour scheme consisting of, at most, three colours plus green. The larger the garden, the larger number of colour schemes which can be employed for different areas or 'rooms' in the garden.

Ideally, we should use together colours from the same areas of the colour spectrum, combining hot colours like reds and oranges or planting cool blues with mauves, but this is not always possible or necessary providing we do not place colours which clash next to one another. Nature never does this, even when employing some of the most vivid hues whether it be in the plant or animal worlds.

YELLOWS

Colour in the garden, even green (though this is not always realized), provides continuity, and it is important to achieve this. Green apart, yellow or yellow variegation occurs in leaves more often than any other colour and therefore offers a greater choice in trees, shrubs, herbaceous including grasses and even climbers. Most people tend to use yellow-leaved specimens individually for contrast with purples and

17

blues; they can be used to even greater effect when grouped together in their many contrasting forms, and will light up an area of the garden as if in sunshine, even on a dull day. Picture the lovely tree *Robinia pseudoacacia* 'Frisia', with its slightly pendant branches heavily clothed with small oval leaves. The golden cut-leaved elder, *Sambucus racemosa* 'Plumosa Aurea' would be a good contrasting shrub with a large-leaved perennial alongside, perhaps the variegated New Zealand flax, *Phormium tenax* 'Variegatum'. A little lower could be the yellow-leaved form of *Choisya ternata*, called 'Sundance', and the pretty and slow-growing Japanese maple, *Acer japonicum* 'Aureum'. Finally, at the foot of the group, another large-leaved perennial, the golden-leaved *Hosta* 'Sum and Substance' would provide contrast with the little gold-striped bamboo *Arundinaria viridistriata* or one of the golden grasses such as *Hakonechloa macra* 'Alboaurea', or *Molinia caerulea* 'Variegata'. In this grouping we have achieved continuity of colour with contrast and variation in leaf form and size.

WHITE

White with a green background will give a similar 'lighting up' effect but this will largely be achieved with flowers. A good background subject would be the shrub *Viburnum plicatum* 'Mariesii', with its horizontal layered branches and white lace-cap flowers. The large-leaved perennial this time could be *Crambe cordifolia* and perhaps a group of arum lilies, *Zantedeschia aethiopica* 'Crowborough'. Additional white could be in the form of white variegated shrubs such as *Cornus sibirica* 'Variegata' or *Aralia elata* 'Variegata' with its elegant arching sprays of pinnate white-edged leaves, and finally a clump of white-edged hostas such as *H.* 'Thomas Hogg'.

Almost any colour can be added to white and is often desirable to relieve any coldness. Purples and pinks work particularly well. For a sunny spot the purple smoke bush, *Cotinus coggygria* 'Royal Purple' would make a lovely background for anything white but especially the rather tender variegated reed, *Arundo donax* 'Variegata'. The purple *Phormium tenax purpureum* would give contrast of form, along with another large-leaved perennial, *Acanthus mollis* 'Latifolius' with its mauve and white flower spikes and perhaps in front the little heuchera, 'Palace Purple'.

In light shade we could add those beautiful shrubs, *Hydrangea aspera* or *H. sargentiana*, with their sumptuous velvety leaves and mauve and white lace-cap flowers. The large-leaved perennial here could be *Rheum palmatum tanguticum*, whose leaves are carmine underneath and tinged red on top. A group of turk's cap lilies, *Lilium martagon*, with their soft pinkish purple flowers, would accentuate this, perhaps together with a drift of *Polygonum bistorta* 'Superbum', with their similarly coloured flowers but contrasting poker shape. For bolder contrast we could use another large-leaved perennial, *Ligularia dentata* 'Desdemona', with its heart-shaped leaves whose stems and undersides are intense purplish red, but we would have to remove its orange flowers later in the summer to maintain our colour scheme. In a sunny spot the leaves would also be tinged with purple on top. If more pink is desirable then one of the more subtly hued pink astilbes could be added.

USING PURPLE

Glaucous blue-grey or grey-green is difficult to mix with ordinary greens but is stunning with purples. In a sunny position, with some of the purple plants just mentioned we could have, for example, a eucalyptus tree such as *Eucalyptus niphophila* or *Eucalyptus*

Veratrum viride, pleating at its finest in the vegetable world.

gunnii, which can be pruned to form a bush. Two more large-leaved perennials, neither of which we should be without, can be included in such a scheme: the semi-tender *Melianthus major*, with its bold serrated leaves, and *Hosta sieboldiana elegans* with its oval, strongly ribbed leaves. The plume poppy, *Macleaya cordata*, is another glaucous large-leaved perennial, its three-lobed leaves, of a similar but less intense hue, are not so good with purples, but the bronzy colouring of its flowers is heightened when it is planted with a fairly recently introduced bronzy grass called *Deschampsia caespitosa* 'Golden Dew'.

Even more beautiful with purple, perhaps, is silver. A purple rheum, for example, would contrast beautifully with an underplanting of the creeping *Lamium maculatum* 'Beacon Silver', and a purple phormium would look stunning with a skirt of the silver filigree foliage of *Artemesia arborescens* or *A. canescens* and perhaps the new heuchera, *H.* 'Snow Storm', with its silvery white leaves and dazzling red flowers. Artemisias and heucheras require reasonable drainage, as do the magnificent silvery thistle-like plants like the cardoon, *Cynara cardunculus*, or *Onopordum acanthium*, both in the 2 m (6 ft) range. Slightly smaller are the eryngiums such as *E. giganteum*. If spiny plants are not to your taste, then *Verbascum olympicum* with its big rosettes of silvery woolly leaves and tall yellow flower spikes, rising to 2.5 m (8 ft), should appeal. Again, it is a plant for a well-drained spot, perhaps in gravel.

We can of course add reds to our purples – subjects like *Crocosmia* 'Lucifer', for example, would be admirable. This would be a change from the norm of mixing reds with oranges and yellows.

SHADES OF GREEN

Yellows and purples are more plentiful than any other colours when it comes to foliage, but we should not forget that there are many diverse and subtle shades of green itself to be exploited, and ever greater variety is supplied by the different textures of leaves. *Rodgersia* (*Astilboides*) *tabularis*, for example, has huge circular leaves of the palest green. These are not only a lovely contrast to the star-shaped crinkly bronze leaves of, say, *Rodgersia podophylla* but are a beautiful foil to the turquoise blue flowers of the Himalayan poppy, *Meconopsis sheldonii*. The ostrich fern, *Matteuccia struthiopteris*, is an equally fresh pale green. The greeny yellow flowers heads of marsh spurge, *Euphorbia palustris*, if planted with them, will heighten the gold of these pale greens like sun shining through them. All would thrive together as they like moisture and dappled shade.

Preferring the same conditions are two more large-leaved perennials, *Smilacina racemosa* and *Aruncus dioicus* (syn. *A. sylvestris*): both have divided leaves and creamy coloured flower plumes. The latter is best used for waterside planting where it is of great value for the variety of form it adds, but the fresh green leaves of *Smilacina racemosa*, looking like some exotic solomon's seal, is more suited to woodland. Although a beautiful and architectural plant, it needs some stronger colours alongside to enhance it, preferably pink and blue or mauve. A Turk's cap lily would

A group of yellow-foliaged plants showing the diversity of leaf shape to be found:
1. *Robinia pseudoacacia* 'Frisia'
2. *Phormium tenax* 'Variegatum'
3. *Sambucus racemosa* 'Plumosa Aurea'
4. *Choisya ternata* 'Sundance'
5. *Acer japonicum* 'Aureum'
6. *Arundinaria viridistriata*
7. *Hosta* 'Sum and Substance'
8. *Hakonechloa macra* 'Alboaurea'.

be ideal here, as would Himalayan poppies (*Meconopsis* spp) or, at a lower level, even in front of the smilacina, could be the salmon-hued *Primula pulverulenta* and the water forget-me-not, *Myosotis scorpioides* 'Mermaid'.

Shady spots

Trachystemon orientale, is the ideal large-leaved perennial for those difficult shady dry spots and makes very good ground cover. It looks most attractive when planted with cranesbills whose finely divided leaves relieve the solidness of those of the trachystemon. Other good companions for it would be *Dicentra formosa*, again with ferny foliage, or the lush-leaved *Dicentra spectabilis* (bleeding heart).

The veratrums are also best when grown in dappled shade, for although they will grow in full sun their splendid pleated foliage often gets scorched. Lilies, especially the turk's cap variety, are again some of the best companions for the bland-flowered veratrums, although a bold group of the black-flowered *Veratrum nigrum* would be quite dramatic on its own.

Matching like with like

Because the foliage of veratrums is so striking, it is best when grouped with other architectural subjects where it would add variety and contrast, plants such as rheums and ligularias, perhaps this time the huge *L. wilsoniana* or *L. veitchiana*, with their big almost triangular leaves. The butter yellow variegated *Polygonum cuspidatum* 'Spectabile', would be a good

Rheum palmatum tanguticum, the leaves tinged purple and blue when young are produced further into the season than other kinds.

background and rodgersias such as *R. podophylla* but especially *R. pinnata* 'Superba' with feathery pink flower spikes, would be suitable additions to such a group. The so-called poke weeds, *Phytolacca americana* and *P. clavigera* seem to succeed best in a fairly open situation, though they will tolerate light shade. Although quite substantial in leaf they are most attractive when closely planted with other things. *P. clavigera* is the better of the two, both for its rose pink flowers and its red stems, and its companions need to be quite bold in order to hold their own against the strong robust shape, but should all be shorter so that it sits among them like a candelabrum. The evergreen bergenias – good forms are *B.* 'Ballawley' or *B.* 'Eric Smith' – would be admirable both for their rose pink flowers in summer and their bronzed leaves in winter and would more or less cover the gap left by the phytolacca at that time. *Bergenia cordifolia* 'Purpurea' is even more colourful in winter than the two varieties cited above, the whole plant turning a purplish red.

While on the subject of bergenias, the most beautiful of all this genus must not be forgotten. The ordinary evergreen kinds just mentioned are perfect for underplanting or on the edge of curved or island beds to give additional emphasis, but *Bergenia ciliata*, though deciduous, is too lovely a plant to be obscured by any others. With its round hairy leaves reaching 30 cm (1 ft) across, it should be given pride of place somewhere in dappled shade, perhaps on the edge of a pool with rodgersias and ligularias for company. The only instance in whch I would use it for underplanting is with a large tree-fern, *Dicksonia antarctica*, or a Chusan palm, *Trachycarpus fortunei*, whose fronds would be held high enough above the bergenia. A shady dell occupied by the former would certainly be a very beautiful sight. An alternative to the bergenia would be the lovely Chatham Island forget me not,

23

Myosotidium hortensia, with its equally large but strongly ribbed round shiny leaves and sprays of little blue flowers.

Bold bulbs

A dell would certainly be the perfect setting for one of the most dramatic perennials, the bulbous giant lily, *Cardiocrinum giganteum*. It is not an easy plant but if you can provide the conditions it needs, that of a very deep acid humus, and you can afford to buy sufficient bulbs of varying ages which will be necessary to give an annual show, then you will be rewarded by a breathtaking experience when your colony or group comes to fruition. Certainly this plant is too much of a showstopper to have its limelight stolen by any lesser ones and as such we cannot seriously consider companions for it unless we simply frame it with something as humble as ferns.

Almost equal in stature though less dramatic than *Cardiocrinum giganteum*, is another bulbous perennial, the eremurus, or foxtail lily. When considering companions for these the main thing to bear in mind is the gap they will leave when finished. The long strap-like leaves are also somewhat untidy and the stately flower spikes need a dark background to set them off. The back of a sunny border is where they are usually planted and because of their stature should be given largish companions. Herbaceous plants such as *Crambe cordifolia* would be fine in summer but an evergreen shrub such as a phormium or yucca would be better, as then the hole left in winter would be less evident. Another important consideration would also be that of colour. The purple *Phormium tenax purpureum*, for example, would make an excellent companion for the largest eremurus, *E. robustus*, with its 3 m (10 ft) high ivory spikes.

Eucomis is another group of dramatic bulbous plants but except in mild regions with good sunshine I consider it to be far more suitable for pot culture (see Chapter 6) as the plants benefit from the extra soil warmth supplied this way.

Some like it hot

There are a few rather tender but interesting large-leaved plants which I would like to include here, because although they share a love of warmth with the species suggested in Chapter 5, they also require drier conditions than the lush, jungly habitat discussed later.

Heat is something which is certainly appreciated by that most extraordinary and exotic-looking of plants, *Beschorneria yuccoides*, looking more like some rain forest bromeliad than a member of the *Amaryllis* family, which it is. This likes to be thoroughly baked and the best way to achieve this is to plant it in a sunny rockery, in paving or in a pot. It is such a dramatic plant when in flower with its 2.5 m (8 ft) arching flower spikes of coral pink bracts and green bells, that it is difficult to mix with other subjects but perhaps the giant mauve-flowered *Echium pinniana* would hold its own here.

The yuccas certainly seem very tolerant of drought. It is said that this is the best way to get both yuccas and phormiums to flower, but I think myself it is more a question of warmth. I also find yuccas most unattractive when not in flower and this is the first thing to remember when considering companions for them. I have found white variegated or white-flowered shrubs the most suitable candidates here; they both detract from the dullness of the foliage of the yucca, and enhance it when in flower. Liking the same conditions of full sun and good drainage, *Crambe cordifolia* would suit, but in an ordinary sunny border with more moisture the white variegated shrubs *Cornus sibirica* 'Variegata' or *Cornus alba* 'Elegantissima' would be better. They could then be combined with such perennials as arum lilies (*Zantedeschia* spp.) and white variegated hostas. Once sufficient white has been provided, warmth could be added to the scheme in the form of pink and purple.

Cautleya spicata, though hardy, is quite exotic-looking, with its deep yellow and maroon bracts and ginger-like foliage. It will grow in sun or dappled shade, and the latter will suit one of the lovelier companions for it. *Lilium canadense* is a very elegant lily with golden yellow trumpets whose mouths have maroon spots. Of similar colouring but with the turk's cap shape is another lily, one of the Bellingham hybrids called 'Shuksan'.

The invaders

The giant hogweed, *Heracleum mantegazzianum*, would be best confined to an island in the middle of a large pond or lake, but if you have some rough woodland then this stately plant with its huge umbrellas of tiny white flowers and enormous cut leaves will soon colonize it. Of lower stature but equally invasive, *Petasites japonicus giganteus* is the ideal ground cover plant for a large area of heavy wet clay in shade. The huge kidney-shaped leaves 1 m (3 ft) across collapse in sun even in boggy soil. Again rough woodland, especially if there is a stream or river, will have its banks covered in the wink of an eye if this is planted on them, any weeds in its path will be smothered.

While on the subject of invasive plants it would be amiss of me not to include here the giant knotweeds. The largest of them, *Polygonum sachalinense*, is not decorative enough for the garden proper but again for rough ground will make a fine show, growing to around the 3.5 m (12 ft) mark. Far lovelier is the smaller cream and butter-yellow variegated *Polygonum cuspidatum* 'Spectabile' at 2–3 m (6–9 ft). But beware, for although the original plant will not seem to spread that rapidly it has the unfortunate habit of sending out long runners which can pop up quite a way from the main clump. Despite this, this plant's beauty, especially in spring when its canes are reddish pink, make it rather desirable. One method of controlling its spread is that used for bamboos, whereby a length of old conveyor belt about 1 m (3 ft) wide is buried around it. The coloration of this knotweed deems it suitable as a companion to a grouping of yellow-leaved or variegated plants (see page 17), but its size dictates that they should be large enough to hold their own with it. Perhaps *Inula magnifica* or the similarly looking but smaller *Buphthalmum speciosum* which would make a nice footnote.

Variations on a theme

Although I mentioned some of the rodgersias earlier these noble plants deserve wider mention. Because of their variety of leaf form and colour, they contrast well not just with other plants but with each other. For example, *Rodgersia tabularis* (syn. *Astilboides tabularis*) with its round pale green leaves could be planted successfully either with *Rodgersia podophylla* with star-shaped bronzy leaves, or with ferns or astilbes. In turn *R. podophylla*, or for that matter *R. pinnata* 'Superba', would fit in well with ferns or astilbes. Near water these species would combine happily with bog primulas and others, but more of that in Chapter 4. *Rodgersia sambucifolia* is not often seen, but is a very attractive and individual plant, quite different in appearance from the other rodgersias in that the pinnate segments are arranged in a half rather than full circle. Given the space, it would be satisfying to grow all these plants, but we could change the partnerships in different areas of the garden.

The ligularias, although not possessing such varied leaf shapes, do have flower spikes of different forms. The dramatic 3 m (10 ft) yellow spires of *Ligularia wilsoniana* with its big green, heavily veined leaves are a real feature of the landscape and even if planted not far from, for example, *Ligularia dentata* 'Desdemona' would not be repetitive as this has candelabra spikes of orange flowers and smooth dark green leaves with purple stems and undersides.

The almost endless variety of size, shape and leaf colour available in the hosta family means that they have a book of their own in this series. I would only suggest a few examples here, with a note that the colour of their leaves should be the prime consideration when choosing companions for them.

The much sought-after *Hosta sieboldiana* 'Frances Williams' with its glaucous grey leaves with greeny gold margins make it a little easier to place than the plain glaucous green kinds; it deserves an important spot as it remains in pristine condition well into the autumn. The bronze-leaved *Rodgersia pinnata* 'Superba' would be a beautiful companion to it, as it is to any of the blue-leaved hostas. These blue-leaved varieties are complemented by a substantial clump of *Heuchera* 'Palace Purple' or even a perimeter of *Ajuga reptans* 'Purpurea' with its little bright blue flowers.

The suggestions I have made for companion planting may seem at first glance a little restrictive, especially in terms of colour, but once the different groupings are brought together the possibilities will be more evident. You may follow them to the letter, but the fun is to experiment until a satisfying result is obtained.

I have so far recommended companions or groupings with which my main aim has been to achieve variety of form and harmony of colour. These plant groups and associations will in themselves be more attractive if installed into a garden with a good framework or bones.

Planting ideas

Herbaceous plants are largely deciduous and so it is essential to incorporate evergreens to avoid undue bareness in winter. Small conifers are often used but are really only suitable where heathers and alpine plants are concerned. The larger growing forms are useful for screening or dividing areas. For our purpose, however, evergreen shrubs are more suitable.

The best method when dealing with beds or borders is to divide them into compartments and shrubs are the best subjects for this. It is not essential that they are all evergreen but the more that are the more attractive the winter picture will be. These shrubs will largely act as a framework to a grouping, and those with coloured foliage – yellow and purple for example – can be incorporated into the groups themselves as previously suggested. Even hedging shrubs such as laurel and elaeagnus can be used but allowed to grow naturally and only pruned with secateurs to keep them in check. If more colour is desirable or if there is not sufficient space to include shrubs in the groupings themselves, the shrubs appropriate to the groupings of herbaceous plants can be used as a background or as dividers instead. For example use a pink camellia for a pink or pink, purple and white group, a *Choisya ternata* for a white or white and cream group, or a yellow rhododendron for a yellow or yellow and white group. If there is insufficient space for shrubs as a backcloth,

Acanthus mollis 'Latifolius'. The flowers surprise the uninitiated by being hard and prickly.

walls or fences can be covered with suitable climbers.

One thing to bare in mind at this stage is that some of the perennials will benefit from light shade and where possible one or two trees should be included. The choice and size of subjects will be dictated by the size of your garden, but division or compartmenting with shrubs informally this way is far more attractive than a continuous run of purely herbaceous material. Another but less obvious advantage is the protection from wind that is given by the shrubs.

Remember that some of the herbaceous perennials die back earlier in the season than others and so should be situated such that they do not leave too obvious a gap. Such plants as rheums or eremurus are usually best placed more to the back of the border.

To a certain extent this bareness can also be avoided by using ground cover plants, which can also give a nice finish to the front of a bed or border. In winter plants like hellebores are especially good as even when their flowers have finished their foliage remains attractive. In spring bulbs can be used between the shrubs or perennials as they will have more or less finished and died back by the time the perennials have developed.

Positioning of herbaceous plants in the border

It is standard practice with beds and borders (even island beds) to place the shortest plants in front and grade up to the tallest at the back. This can sometimes look a trifle monotonous, understandably one does not want to hide any plants from view, but this need not be the case if the right kind of taller plants are placed in more forward positions: plants with 'see through' type foliage which may be feathery or ferny such as fennel and even the taller grasses. Remember also that some

plants, although tall in flower, sometimes have a low-growing basal clumps of leaves. By occasionally using taller subjects this way we relieve the regularity.

It is also important to be able to use large subjects sometimes near the front of borders to emphasize their shape, and where hard landscaping is concerned to be able to use their foliage to soften any hard lines by breaking them up. Where beds or borders are fronted by grass, large subjects should be far enough back that their leaves do not flop over the edge and become a nuisance when the lawn is mown. Where borders meet gravel or paving this does not matter; in fact where gravel is concerned a few plants over-spilling on to it gives a very attractive and natural effect.

Arranging perennials

One of the advantages of perennials is that they can be moved at almost any time of the year, unlike trees and shrubs which can only be moved in the dormant season. Providing they are well watered before being dup up, and lifted with a reasonable amount of soil and replanted immediately they should not suffer. It is wise however to avoid moving them on hot sunny days, when many plants are apt to wilt in the heat, or when they are at vigorous stages of growth and their leaves expanding.

This enables us to rearrange them should we wish to experiment with new associations, an advantage so far as time is concerned. A garden is never *finished* in the true sense as most of us are continually making changes even if they are only subtle ones. We may discover new plants or tire of old ones. Change is desirable as our interest and enthusiasm is thereby retained. Even the greatest plants people of our time have worked this way and spent many years achieving a personally satisfying result. The suggestions I have given should be considered as basic guidelines and further inspiration should be sought by visiting some of the great gardens and plant collections around the country. This and reading are the best ways of self educating, the greatest benefits of which are the reduction in mistakes and so a saving of time.

When visiting gardens make notes of plant associations or groupings which particularly please you, it is very easy to forget such things especially when plants can have such long and difficult names. If you take photographs remember to note down the names of the plants you have snapped; there will not always be someone who can identify them for you.

Planning your garden

I have already stressed the value of such things as water in the relative chapters, but I feel it important to give mention especially for the garden novices amongst you, as to some practical points when considering the design or general layout of gardens, which if nothing else will save time and error. As I have already mentioned trees and shrubs are not as easily moved as herbaceous plants especially when they are well established. Therefore careful consideration should be given before planting these things which will form the framework or 'bones' of the garden.

The best method is to do a scale drawing as the size and shape of a garden can be very deceptive when you are in it. Note the direction your garden faces. This will affect the amount of sun and shade you will have and will influence the number of trees (if any) you may choose or require, remember many plants benefit from partial shade.

You should also at this stage consider your boundaries as they should be thought of as part of the framework. Hedges are the most attractive form of boundary but take several years to establish, especially if they are required to be a reasonable height to give wind protection. Gardens vary tremendously so far as shelter is concerned and exposed gardens should have the shelter established before serious planting is undertaken.

The next decision is the layout of your paths, beds and borders, water features and so on, after which you are then (and not before) at the stage to consider your planting plans.

The simplest method is to think of the plants as consisting of four layers as follows: 1 – trees. 2 – Shrubs. 3 – Herbaceous plants. 4 – Ground cover, and they should really be planted in that order.

If your garden is not on a level site this can be an advantage as further interest can be created by accentuating the different levels with steps, and the lower levels or hollows which are usually the dampest used for the more moisture loving plants or as a natural looking situation for a pond.

Whatever the size and shape of your garden it will be far more interesting if it is planted in such a way that it cannot *all* be seen at a single glance. This is easily achieved by winding paths and strategically placing large shrubs for example to mask your view and thereby arouse interest and curiosity so that new or different vistas appear one by one.

It is worth some time and effort in carefully planning all these things as the final result will be vastly more satisfactory than a mere jumble of plants. Individual plants may be very beautiful in themselves but it is the context in which they are used (i.e. their companions and siting etc) within the whole which can display them to best effect and whereby their full beauty can be appreciated.

CHAPTER 4

Large-leaved perennials and water

Water, more than any other element, adds life, interest and beauty to the garden. The sound as well as the sight of it, especially on a warm summer's day, is both peaceful and relaxing.

Some of the most attractive features to be found in gardens are those assocated with water. It is such a versatile element, in formal use as a fountain or trickle from a statue, to informal natural features – a dramatic waterfall or cascade, a bubbling stream or a 'secret' silent pool. In whichever of these forms it appears it should always form the focal point of the garden and as such there should be somewhere close by where you can sit and enjoy it.

Water is of particular importance where large-leaved perennials are concerned as so many of them require the conditions it creates to sustain them and enable them to grow to their full glory and perfection. It is also beside water that their full beauty can be appreciated as it is such a natural setting for them. A variety of plants with large foliage planted on the margins of water give a lush, luxuriant feel and the reflections they cast in the water add further beauty and enhancement.

Water features

I will always remember the very first time I saw the Great Waterfall at Chatsworth House. At the foot of the fall on either side are two great clumps of gunnera which receive the spray from it. Waterfalls and cascades are the most beautiful and spectacular of water features, whether natural or man-made, and with the addition of lush and luxuriant planting around them can be breathtaking. Vegetation is naturally rich around them because of the moisture and humidity that is created. A crashing waterfall may not be to everyone's taste but a silent pool can be just as beautiful.

One of the best examples of water gardens that I have seen is Longstock Park, in southern England. It is a large flat piece of land, dissected by a series of lagoons and channels crossed by plank bridges. The banks and margins of the water are richly planted with a wide range of foliage and flowering plants – one tiny lagoon is fringed entirely with hostas. The plantings are broken by the turf paths which occasionally come to the water's edge. It is important whether you have a lake, pond, river or stream that you can reach the water in this way, as then you can fully appreciate at close quarters the beauty of the plants on the margins.

Whatever the size of your garden ideas such as these can be used from such places. You do not have to possess a lake in order to grow a gunnera, but where space is limited, an alternative would be the umbrella plant, *Peltiphyllum peltatum*, or perhaps a rheum.

Whether by an informal pond or stream, or a formal terrace pool or swimming pool, large-leaved

A bold clump of *Gunnera manicata* backed here by a magnificent red Japanese maple lit by the sun.

perennials can be used to good effect. On a formal terrace, large pots on the paving with plants with bold shapes like acanthus or ligularias and hostas would do much to enhance and relieve the flatness of the area. In the pool itself pots or baskets of water dock (*Rumex*) or arum lilies alongside irises and so on would be reflected in the water and break up the straight edges.

Large areas of paving round an outdoor swimming pool should be broken with beds for plants or a collection of pots, the number depending on the dimensions of the area. Here, I feel, a slightly more exotic feel would be appropriate and more exciting, and a combination of large-leaved perennials and hardy but tropical-looking plants like palms, bamboos and phormiums would certainly achieve this (see Chapter 5).

Just as owners of small gardens should not be deterred from growing large plants, neither should

Pots or baskets with bold foliage enhance and soften formal ponds by breaking up the hard straight edges.
1. Bog iris
2. *Zantedeschia aethiopica*
3. *Senecio smithii*
4. *Caltha polypetala*.

they deprive themselves of a water feature. Once you have introduced a water feature into the garden you will never want to be without it. It is so easy these days – with plastic and butyl liners a pond can be installed in a matter of hours, unlike the days when ponds had to be made of concrete or puddled clay and even then were prone to leaks.

The range of waterside habitats

When water is incorporated into the garden's design it greatly expands the range of plants that can be grown, and these fall into several categories.

There are, first, the plants which actually live in or under the water, such as the water lilies, but as we are dealing here specifically with large-leaved perennials, the only subjects which will apply are those which normally grow in just a little water, and are usually close to the banks – plants like *Senecio smithii*, giant water dock (*Rumex hydrolapathum*) or giant marsh marigold (*Caltha polypetala*). In natural or informal ponds these would be planted out in the shallow water, but in formal ponds could be grown in pots or baskets and would therefore help to mask some of the concrete or stonework.

Next are the bog plants, subjects which do not like their crowns submerged but which must have permanently moist or wet conditions. The British native butterbur, *Petasites hybridus*, and its Japanese equivalent, *P. japonicus giganteus*, are rampant indeed. Less invasive is the umbrella plant, *Peltiphyllum peltatum* which, if planted at the water's edge, will grow both up the bank and down into the water. The arum lily, *Zantedeschia aethiopica*, in its hardiest form 'Crowborough' can also be grown in the water providing it is planted at least 15 cm (6 in) below the surface.

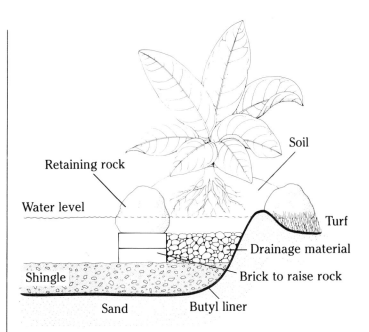

A section of a marginal bed at a poolside.

Then there are those most magnificent of waterside plants, the bog arums, *Lysichiton americanum* (yellow), *L. camtschatcensis* (white) and the gunneras, *G. manicata* and *G. scabra* (*G. chilensis*). I must stress here that these plants would be happy in natural boggy conditions where the water flows through the soil, but when a bog area has been artificially created, such as with a butyl liner, it is necessary first to have a layer of drainage material about 15–20 cm (6–8 in) thick of broken brick or gravel (Fig. 5), and to replace the soil every three to four years as it eventually becomes sour and would rot the roots of even bog plants such as these.

Lysichitons and gunneras can also be planted in our final waterside setting, the damp border, but may not grow quite as luxuriantly as where their roots can reach down to water.

33

The damp border is where ligularia, rodgersia, rheum, filipendula and aruncus will all flourish. Most will also benefit from a little shade to prevent scorching or wilting of the leaves. They can all be planted on the water's edge, and indeed are more attractive there, but they must either be planted in marginal beds or outside the pond liner. Where there is natural water they should be above the flood plain as they will not tolerate either being submerged or having water stagnating around their roots. The ground therefore should be built up before planting where necessary to prevent this happening.

A flower for every season

Although the large-leaved perennials suitable for association with water are chosen predominantly for the variety of leaf shapes, we should not forget the interest and attraction by way of flowers they also supply.

Early in the spring the floral rosettes of petasites emerge before the leaves; the strange frilled flower heads which sit on the ground are very popular with flower arrangers. A month or so later the lysichitons produce their magnificent yellow or white spathes as the leaves begin to emerge, these are beautiful when reflected in the water. Incidentally, there is a hybrid (as yet unnamed) between *L. americanum* and *L. camtschatcensis*, which has even larger leaves, up to 2 m (6 ft) of a lovely glaucous pale green, and handsome creamy coloured spathes which can be as much as 45 cm (18 in) high. About the same time the umbrella plant, *Peltiphyllum peltatum*, pushes up its little pink flower heads on tall hairy stalks, a rather strange sight, and these are almost over before the leaves begin to appear.

Colourful and decorative in summer are the fluffy flower spikes of the rhubarb-like rheums. Those of the ordinary *Rheum palmatum* are creamy white but those of *R. p.* 'Atrosanguineum' are a lovely cherry red. Both top 2 m (6 ft). The flowers of *Aruncus dioicus* are also creamy white through the summer, but less fluffy and more like an astilbe. Filipendulas have similar but much flatter-topped heads; in *F. camtschatica* they are ivory white, but in *F. palmata* 'Rubra' they are a glistening rosy red.

The flowers of ligularias, which appear later in high summer, are predominantly orange or yellow of varying shades but very variable in form. Those of *L. dentata* 'Desdemona' or *L. dentata* 'Gregynog Gold', for example, are of candelabra form, while those of *L. przewalskii* 'The Rocket', *L. veitchiana* or *L. wilsoniana* are tall spikes, slender in the case of 'The Rocket'.

More daisy-like flowers, but this time large and yellow, are produced by *Inula magnifica* in a candelabra-like spike 2.5 m (8 ft) high above the huge paddle-shaped leaves. The rodgersias again provide more astilbe-like, feathery plumes, ivory in *R. pinnata* 'Elegans' and brilliant pink in *R. pinnata* 'Superba', an effective tone with its bronzy leaves.

In late summer the arum lilies (*Zantedeschia*) always stand out, their white spathes with yellow spadixes backed by their shining dark green leaves. For flower arrangers the variety 'Green Goddess' with its green and white flowers would be a must.

Down almost in the water *Senecio smithii* is a very decorative subject when carrying its yellow-eyed white daisies, and the giant water dock, *Rumex hydrolapathum*, produces its brownish pink flowers in late summer.

A successful trio of form and colour – the blue-leaved *Hosta tokudama* backed by (LEFT) *Ligularia dentata* 'Desdemona' and red primulas.

Although not at all colourful the huge flowers spikes or, more descriptively, seed heads, of the gunneras are very architectural and dramatic, and those of *G. scabra* (*G. chilensis*) are retained well into the autumn, making quite a feature on the landscape.

Effective planting

When planting up a pond or stream side, remember as well as combining other waterside plants, to use large-leaved perennials of both contrasting shape, colour and texture together. The huge paddle-shaped leaves of *Lysichiton americanum*, for example, would be a good contrast of shape and texture with those of *Gunnera manicata* and yet would hold their own. Next to the lysichiton could be *Rodgersia podophylla* which would give a further contrast of form, colour and texture with its star-shaped, crinkly bronze leaves.

To give height again we could then have either *Filipendula palmata* 'Rubra' or *F. camtschatica* (syn. *F. gigantea*), or *Aruncus dioicus* (syn. *A. sylvestris*), whose pale green divided leaves would contrast well with those of *Ligularia dentata* 'Desdemona', which are kidney-shaped, dark green and purple underneath. A drift of arum lilies, *Zantedeschia aethiopica* 'Crowborough', with their white sails would be set off by the purple and finally a carpet of *Primula pulverulenta* with their salmony pink flowers.

The lovely bog primulas come in various colours from white to purple, the bog irises in even greater variety of colour. The astilbes, with their fluffy flower spikes and ferny leaves, contrast well with the perpendicular outline of the iris.

Drifts of one type of plant by the waterside are far more effective and attractive than a jumble of different ones; where space is limited reduce the variety rather than the numbers of each plant. If you study plants in the wild you will see that they adopt these habits naturally. In Africa, for example, arum lilies (*Zantedeschia aethiopica*) colonize the banks of rivers and streams. In Britain the native butterbur (*Petasites hybridus*) does the same. So in a way we are simply copying nature! Obviously something as large as a gunnera could only be massed by a lake, but certainly three rheums could be planted together by a reasonably sized pond. Bold groups of plants like ligularias will need to be planted in numbers to give a massed effect but the individual clumps can, and indeed should, be divided occasionally to increase the size of the patch and also to maintain the health of the plant. Peltiphyllums, on the other hand, will naturally expand to form a colony and therefore can be left alone. Do not forget that hostas or *Inula magnifica*, although usually associated with a border, will do well by the waterside.

One of the greatest advantages of having water in the garden is that it is not only attractive in itself but it increases the beauty of many plants that can be associated with it. The great number and variety of large-leaved perennials that we have to choose from for use in this situation means that we need never tire of what we have or grow short of ideas for new schemes or changes.

A wide diversity of leaf shape and form by the waterside:
1. *Lysichiton americanum*
2. *Rodgersia pinnata* 'Superba'
3. *Ligularia dentata* 'Desdemona'
4. *Zantedeschia aethiopica*
5. *Peltiphyllum peltatum*
6. *Gunnera manicata*
7. *Aruncus sylvestris* (*dioicus*)
8. Bamboo.

CHAPTER 5

The tropical touch

It is large leaves above all that convey that air of tropical lushness that we usually associate with warmer climes. When thinking of somewhere as exotic the West Indies, we may be forgiven for first visualizing the dazzling colours of such exotic blooms as hibiscus and orchids, but it is also the leafy lushness of these places, the bananas, gingers and palms, which completes the picture – together, of course, with the wonderful sand, sea and sunshine.

We cannot reproduce the climate, except under glass, but you may be surprised how exotic a picture can be painted, even in an uncertain and relatively cool climate. Believe it or not, it is possible to create the kind of scene where, on a hot summer's day, you may be seen sitting in the shade of the banana or palm tree with the flower of a hibiscus in your hair (or on your hat), dangling your toe in a pool to be tickled by the root of the water hyacinth, while the bamboo rustles in the gentle breeze which carries the intoxicating scent of the datura!

Exotic-looking plants seem to have the effect of making it seem warmer than it really is. Another of their great qualities is that they prolong the period of interest. Come late summer, and the traditional bedding plants are beginning to look jaded, dry and frazzled, the exotics are at the peak of their perfection, still fresh and making vigorous growth, which in most cases continues until the frosts. I use the term 'exotic' here loosely, for I am speaking of plants that are merely exotic in appearance not necessarily in origin.

Rodgersia pinnata **making a strong contrast to the lovely golden grass** *Hakonechloa macra variegata.*

The nineteenth-century innovators

With the introduction of lots of newly discovered plants, the fashion of so called sub-tropical gardening arose, involving the planting out in summer of many exotic plants kept under glass in winter. A great industry arose to satisfy the demand both for plants and conservatories, or Winter Gardens as they were called. Mistakes were made by people at the time due to lack of knowledge and experience of the plants, but we have of course since learnt and in the following pages I shall only recommend plants that are either hardy (though exotic looking), or in a few cases frost tender but which still thrive making vigorous growth outdoors in summer. An exotic looking garden can be created without the tender subjects, but if you have a frost-free conservatory or greenhouse and can accommodate them they will do much to enhance your garden.

For anyone looking for a change who is thoroughly bored by traditional forms of gardening with the usual herbaceous and shrub borders, roses and clematis scrambling over pergolas, potted geraniums and hanging baskets of petunias, then the sub-tropical look is for you. Say goodbye to the days of backbreaking trudgery, hours of weeding, staking, pruning, deadheading and planting of countless annuals. Dust the deck chair and prepare it for the summer, for it will be thoroughly used – weather permitting – in an 'exotic' garden. The plants may be unusual, but they are easy to grow, and a garden of this type requires far less maintenance than a traditional one.

The foundations

Generally, because the large-leaved perennials only occupy the lower planting levels, it is necessary to add structure, in this case not just trees or shrubs but palms, bamboos, bananas etc. – a stark contrast to a traditional garden. But first it is important to create the kind of setting in which such exotics will thrive and which suits them aesthetically. Shelter is paramount, as large leaves of any kind become tattered when battered by wind and their beauty destroyed.

In large gardens, tall, preferably evergreen hedges should be grown; in small ones, walls or fences can be topped with trellis covered with fine plastic mesh or evergreen climbers such as ivy.

The second consideration is water. A joy in any garden, it is, I feel, an essential feature in a sub-tropical setting, even if only a small pond or stream with the water splashing over rocks or cobbles. Remember, when deciding where the water will be, that it should be a focal point of the garden and as such there should be somewhere close by for you to sit and enjoy it.

Next come the hard structural elements: paths and paved areas. Never lead a path straight to an area of interest, but curve and twist it, diverting it with large shrubs or clumps of bamboo so that interest and curiosity is aroused. Even in small gardens mystery can be achieved this way. A point of good garden design is that you should never be able to take in or view a whole area at once, but that it should be revealed little by little.

A patio does not have to be the usual paving of stone slabs or bricks. Why not have wooden decking? It is far more comfortable to walk on and very much in keeping with this type of planting. It is also easy to maintain and no more expensive than, say, York stone or old stock bricks. It can be used in a totally informal setting such as by a lake or in a formal area around a swimming pool. Remember, however, to take into account the style or period of the house it would be connected with. These same rules would apply when choosing a conservatory.

Your outdoor furniture should, of course, first and foremost be comfortable. Style is very personal, but furniture of a contemporary or 'Colonial' design is probably more appropriate for this kind of garden and white, although less practical, does add a tropical note.

White is often associated with hot countries, especially for walls and buildings, where it is used to reflect the sun's heat. Certainly it would be appropriate to have white walls around a patio area or swimming pool. Exotic-looking plants in large tubs or terracotta pots would stand out well against the white walls (see also Chapter 6).

There are lots of natural construction materials available now which should be used more often. There are, for example, some lovely white and coloured Italian cobbles to be had which could be used in or out of water. Beds of plants, especially those of an exotic nature, look very attractive when covered with cobbles, when adjoining patio areas or swimming pools. They give a clean modern look ideal for contemporary settings and complement both paving and wooden decking. They are often used, along with gravel, in oriental designs.

Gravel comes in a number of varieties and is probably the best material to use for covering the

A Mediterranean feel can be created at the poolside with hardy exotics and large-leaved perennials:
1. Bamboo – *Phyllostachus aurea*
2. Palm – *Trachycarpus fortunei*
3. *Hosta sieboldiana elegans*
4. *Phormium tenax* 'Variegatum'
5. *Ligularia dentata* 'Desdemona'.

41

bottom of artificial ponds, extending out of the water to form a beach – sand is attractive and comfortable but, I think, impractical in view of the wind, even in sheltered spots.

Several different kinds of rock are available and large smooth boulders can be very decorative.

Other items, such as barbecues, will be added attractions, but I should like to mention one latest innovation: the 'hot tub', surely appropriate here in terms of both the plants and the climate.

In view of the plumbing and convenience in reaching it, it should be situated relatively close to the house. It could for example be installed in an area of wooden decking where it could be easily reached and the lush tropical setting appreciated from the warm water. Hot tubs, though expensive to buy and install are thereafter reasonable to run and maintain. One of their greatest assets is that they can be used all year round, and they are terrific fun for families with children. They originated from the United States where they are very popular.

Creating the exotic look

TEMPERATE TREES WITH A TROPICAL LOOK

The trees and shrubs described below are perfect companions to large-leaved perennials. When planted with them they make even familiar things such as hostas look more unusual. Large-leaved perennials are in themselves a trifle exotic, but when mixed with such things as palms and bamboos their lushness is accentuated, and they take on a totally new look.

Rodgersia tabularis (Astilboides tabularis) is a plant of great beauty and grace; at the peak of perfection it requires careful culture.

It seems only natural to begin with the largest things, as these are normally the 'bones' of the garden and as such their position needs careful consideration.

There are few trees of an exotic nature, but as space in most gardens normally only permits a few, this is of little consequence. They all have large leaves which gives them an exotic or sub-tropical look and are mentioned in order of merit.

The Indian horse chestnut, *Aesculus indica*, is a medium-sized tree to about 10 m (30 ft) possessing smooth dark green seven-lobed leaves (those of the common kinds are much coarser). It produces large panicles of pink flowers in late summer. The Japanese poplar, *Populus lasiocarpa*, has 30 cm (1 ft) long heart-shaped leaves with red veins and stalks and is of rather open habit and is also of medium height. The familiar tree of Heaven, *Ailanthus altissima*, with its pinnate leaves would be too big for most gardens, but if pollarded each winter (i.e. cut to within 15 cm (6 in) of the ground), can be accommodated more easily and will produce larger leaves if treated this way (up to 90 cm (3 ft) long).

The same treatment should be given to the foxglove tree, *Paulownia imperialis* (syn. *P. tomentosa*), which is a fine contrast, having almost unlobed leaves 60 cm (2 ft) or more across (if pollarded). It must, however, have full sun and shelter from strong wind.

The eucalyptuses are valuable for being evergreen. One of the best is *E. niphophila*, the snow gum, with broad sickle-shaped leaves and trunk marbled cream, grey and green. A fast-growing, tall but light tree to approximately 20 m (60 ft).

The Chilean fire tree, *Embothrium coccineum*, will be more of a large shrub for most of us, and is dazzling when clothed with its orange-red flowers in early summer. It is evergreen and somewhat tender, though the variety *E. c. lanceolatum* 'Norquinco Valley' is said to be hardier.

PALMS AND BAMBOOS

The first of our truly exotic subjects is the Chusan or windmill palm, *Trachycarpus fortunei*. Though slow growing it will eventually reach some 6 m (20 ft) or more, and is one of the largest of exotic-looking trees that can be grown in a cool climate. Sometimes it is to be seen in ordinary plantings, where it looks quite out of place, but with equally foreign-looking subjects such as bamboos and phormiums, it is in perfect keeping. Happy in sun or dappled shade, the large fan-like segmented leaves 90 cm (3 ft) across are very distinctive and handsome, suiting both informal and formal situations, such as paved areas or alongside swimming pools along with other architectural plants. It can also be grown in a large pot, though this will slow its rate of growth as it likes to be kept permanently moist at the roots. Although hardy, it should be positioned out of strong winds which will otherwise dishevel its appearance; it is worthwhile going to some trouble to keep a Chusan palm in good fetter as it is undoubtedly one of the best for producing an exotic effect outside a tropical climate. Although expensive to procure, it is well worth the expenditure in view of the charm added to a planting. There *are* a few other palms which have proved to be reasonably hardy, but they do not have the rate of growth of the Chusan palm, and would therefore take even longer to attain a reasonable size.

Next in importance for effect after the Chusan palm I would place the bamboos. Despite their exotic appearance the majority of the kinds available are quite hardy, originating from eastern Asia and Japan. Their graceful character and beauty, especially when planted by water makes them indispensable. Because of their upright habit and grass-like appearance they are also a lovely contrast to the more solid or horizontal forms of other plants. They vary mainly in the size of the leaf and the colour of their canes and their height can be from as little as 60 cm (2 ft) to 7 m (20 ft) or so. Many grow much taller in their native habitat.

One of the smallest but most colourful is *Arundinaria viridistriata*, growing only 60–90 cm (2–3 ft), its leaves are striped lemon yellow. It should be cut to ground level at the end of each winter to produce the best growth the following season.

For small gardens or containers *Arundinaria murielae* and *A. nitida* at about 2–3 m (6–10 ft) are similar to each other and easy to grow.

Sasa palmata 'Nebulosa', though only 2 m (6 ft) high is distinct in having much larger leaves than most bamboos at 30–40 cm (12–16 in) long. It is, however, rather invasive and best confined to containers in smaller gardens.

The taller kinds, growing up to 6 m (20 ft) or so, more in warmer countries, usually belong to the *Phyllostachys* group. *P. mitis*, *P. aurea* and *P. nigra* are the ones usually available. The first two are similar of yellowish green coloration, but *P. nigra* has jet black canes making it more desirable and decorative. These big bamboos need shelter from strong winds to do their best.

PHORMIUMS AND CORDYLINES

Of the New Zealand flax, *Phormium tenax*, the plain green form is the hardiest. The stiff fans of sword-like leaves 2 m (6 ft) high are overtopped several feet by the architectural if not very colourful flower spikes in good summers. The creamy yellow variegated *P. t.* 'Variegatum', and the purple *P. t. purpureum* of the same proportions are a little less hardy. The smaller *P. cookianum* forms variously coloured pink purple cream and green with more lax foliage are even more tender and are probably only suitable for containers which can be wintered under glass. All phormiums like full sun.

The cordylines or inappropriately named 'cabbage' palms, like the phormiums are valuable for the additional variety of form they introduce into this type of garden.

The hardiest, *C. australis*, has a fountain of narrow leaves about 1 m (3 ft) across which eventually rises on a tall trunk. The very handsome smaller dark purple-leaved *C. a. atropurpurea* is sadly too tender for an outdoor life but makes a super container plant for the conservatory.

DECORATIVE SHRUBS

Aralia cachemirica, being completely deciduous, is classed as a perennial and included in Chapter 7, but *A. elata* produces tall woody spiny stems clothed with whorls of huge pinnate leaves about 70 cm (2½ ft) long, giving a lush appearance especially when planted in groups. There are white and yellow varie-gated forms, *A. e.* 'Variegata' and *A. e.* 'Aureo-variegata' respectively. They are both slower growing and expensive to procure. Aralias like dappled shade. *Fatsia japonica*, often incorrectly called the castor-oil plant, is very handsome with its big lobed shiny ever-green leaves. Often sold as a house plant it is much happier in a shady spot.

Less familiar is the loquat, *Eriobotrya japonica*, which has long crinkly serrated evergreen leaves. It can be grown free standing or as a wall shrub. In hot summers it will produce small orange fruits which are an acquired taste.

Most of you will have seen *Magnolia grandiflora* with its almost rubber tree-like dark green shiny ever-green leaves, but rarely seen and more beautiful and refined is the evergreen *Magnolia delavayi* which has larger grey-green leaves. Two attractive but deciduous magnolias, even rarer, are *M. tripetala* and *M. macro-phylla*, the largest leaved of all magnolias with thin papery leaves to 60 cm (2 ft) long.

For shade are two sumptuous and exotic-looking hydrangeas, *H. aspera* and *H. sargentiana*. Both are similar in that they have velvety leaves and mauve and white lace-cap flowers. *H. aspera* is probably the best as it is bushier, (*H. sargentiana* is inclined to become leggy) and of darker coloration.

Other more familiar shrubs such as camellias, pieris and mahonia are all evergreen and associate well with tropical-looking plants.

EXOTIC CLIMBERS

Clematis armandii should be grown more often. Though less showy than some in flower, its large dark green shiny sickle-shaped evergreen leaves deserve space in any garden. Similar but smaller in leaf is the exotic *Lapageria rosea* with large waxy rosy-red bells unfortunately far too tender except for the mildest gardens.

Almost as exotic looking but hardy is *Campsis taglia-buana* 'Madame Galen' with ferny foliage and large, orangey-red trumpet flowers.

TENDER PLANTS

Some of the tender plants I have selected are perennials, but all have large and handsome leaves, and although an exotic-looking garden can be achieved without them, their inclusion will add great beauty and interest with little extra trouble, especially for those who possess a conservatory or greenhouse. These plants will need to be moved under glass from about mid autumn until late spring, and kept frost-free at about 7°–10°C (45°–50°F).

We all have our favourites and mine, since I first dis-covered it, has been the great Abyssinian banana, *Ensete ventricosum* (*Musa ensete*). Its leaves are huge, beating even the great gunnera for area of leaf. It has to be grown from seed as it does not produce offsets like other bananas, but once germinated these will grow into 1 m (3 ft) plants in six months. Of a much stockier build than most bananas, its thick leaves with their striking red midrib are much less prone to laceration by the wind. It is a very fast grower – in 18 months it will reach 3 m (10 ft) in height if regularly potted on and well fed and watered. By then it will have leaves about 2 m (6 ft) long and 45 cm (18 in) wide. Ultimately it will reach 6 m (20 ft) in height with leaves 4.5 m (14 ft) long by 75 cm (2½ ft) wide, but it would have to be planted out to achieve this. It would then be necessary before the first frost to cut off its leaves, wrap the trunk generously in straw and cover it with sheets of corrugated iron to keep it dry. Alternatively, of course, when it became too big to move indoors, one could easily replace it with a smaller specimen, which, after all, would only cost the price of a packet of seed. This may all seem a great deal of trouble, but the visual effect of such a plant is staggering, and visitors will rub their eyes in astonishment.

There is one other so-called hardy banana, *Musa basjoo*, the Japanese banana. This can be grown permanently out of doors in sheltered or town gardens in mild areas, though I recommend wrapping its trunk in bracken in case of a severe winter, but even when cut down by frost it will usually shoot again from the ground. Although a tall-growing kind it is very slender, with the more usual papery leaves which tear very easily. Its comparative hardiness is to be commended, and it would be a good candidate for a sheltered spot.

Of similar appearance, leaf-wise, to the bananas but of smaller stature are the cannas. Their foliage reaches the 2 m (6 ft) mark while their flowers add another 45 cm (18 in) or so. One of the most beautiful is *Canna×generalis* 'Wyoming', valued on account of its dark purple leaves. The flowers of apricot orange, reminiscent of a gladiolus, are a trifle garish for my taste, but the foliage is a stunning contrast to the glaucous grey serrated, divided leaves of *Melianthus*

major. This combination of foliage is probably one of the choicest that can be made, and would be a high spot in any exotic-style garden. Another equally desirable canna, a little taller at 3 m (10 ft), is *C. iridiflora ehrmanii*. This has huge banana-like leaves 1 m (3 ft) long (green this time) and elegant drooping spikes of rose-coloured flowers. A beautiful companion for this would be *Ricinus communis* 'Gibsonii', a purple-leaved form of the true castor-oil plant. This is an annual which has to be raised from seed sown in the greenhouse in late winter and planted out in late spring.

Most cannas have to be treated rather like dahlias, the tubers lifted in late autumn and dried off in a frost-proof place. They then need to be potted up in early spring and given a little heat, about 15°C (60°F) in the greenhouse to start them into growth to be planted out after the last frosts. *Canna iridiflora ehrmanii*, however, when lifted, should simply be potted up in fresh soil and kept with the other cannas to be planted out with them the following spring.

For sheer exotica, even the cannas are beaten by the daturas. These fast-growing shrubs with their soft downy leaves are an absolute show-stopper when hung with their huge trumpet-shaped blooms. The one usually seen is *Datura cornigera*, which has semi-double white flowers 20 cm (8 in) long with (especially at night) an intoxicating scent. There are other varieties to be had, in shades of cream, pink and orange. All are easy to grow providing they are fed and watered regularly; they strike easily from cuttings and usually flower in their first year. Always keep them in their containers, re-potting or top-dressing annually and keep cool but frost-free, 7–10°C (45–50°F), in winter. Hard prune in early spring to

Cana×generalis 'Wyoming', a tender perennial, valued for its dark purple leaves.

ensure good flowering the following season. Daturas make lovely patio subjects, but if put in the garden proper their pots should be sunk in the ground. They prefer light shade to full sun, which tends to wilt the foliage.

The gingers are another group of exotic flowered plants. The herbaceous foliage consists of canes to about 2 m (6 ft) with opposite rows of long fleshy leaves, which are topped with spikes of almost orchid-like blooms. The most beautiful is *Hedychium gardnerianum*, which has yellow petals with orange stamens in a 20 cm (8 in) long spike. This can only be planted out permanently in very mild areas, where it will be deciduous; otherwise it should be kept in a tub and moved to the conservatory or greenhouse for the winter. There are other similar varieties, such as *H. coccineum* 'Tara', which is hardier, but the hardiest of all is *H. forrestii*. Although deciduous, this is probably the tallest-growing kind, producing 2.5 m (8 ft) canes topped with 15 cm (6 in) spikes of flowers with white petals and orange stamens. When it dies down in the autumn its roots should be covered with a thick mulch.

Although there are some hardy forms of hibiscus, they are by no means as flamboyant and exotic looking as the tropical ones. There is, however, one exception: *Hibiscus moscheutos*. Unlike the tropical kinds, which are evergreen, this is deciduous, in fact, really herbaceous, the stems dying back to the ground each winter. The flowers, which are 15 cm (6 in) across, are spectacular, and come in either red, pink or white according to variety. My favourite, the red form, is 'Southern Belle'. These can be planted out permanently in a sunny position preferably against a wall, but must be given a thick mulch in winter. Their only drawback is that they are late to flower, usually not until the end of the summer, but they are surely a must on account of their very exotic appearance.

A true shrub is *Tibouchina urvilliana* (syn. *T. semidecandra*). The angular stems are clothed with 8 cm (3 in) ovate leaves which are covered in fine white pubescent hairs. The flowers, which are like those of an African violet, are an almost electric blue, 5 cm (2 in) across and freely produced later in the summer. It requires to be kept in the conservatory or greenhouse in winter and when put out for summer should be placed in dappled shade.

Returning to foliage now, the very beautiful lobed leaves of the rice paper plant, *Tetrapanax papyriferus* are 60 cm (2 ft) across, rather the shape of *Fatsia japonica*, and are covered in a fine white down. It can be left out all year but will be deciduous, so it would be better to overwinter it under glass so that it will add instant beauty when put out in late spring. Light shade is preferable, though it will tolerate full sun, but the leaves will be smaller. It it gets too leggy it can be cut down and will shoot from base or below ground.

The tree ferns always attract attention and admiration, the hardiest of which is *Dicksonia antarctica*. A large specimen, which can be 3 m (10 ft) across, is breathtaking. Even small specimens are difficult and expensive to acquire but well worth the effort. They like a shady spot and must be kept moist at all times. The big crown of fronds begins at ground level and gradually forms (after several years) a trunk, hence its name. They are too precious to risk losing by leaving

A bed in a paved area within a walled garden can be planted up with bold leaved perennials and other architectural plants, for a clean, modern and Mediterranean look.
1. Palm (*Trachycarpus fortunei*)
2. *Acanthus mollis* 'Latifolius'
3. *Ligularia dentata* 'Desdemona'
4. *Phormium tenax* 'Variegatum'.
5. Fig (*Ficus carica*)

out all winter, and should be grown in tubs so that they can be moved indoors at the approach of frost.

My last subject is a very beautiful variegated reed, *Arundo donax* 'Variegata' – along with *Aralia elata* 'Variegata', I consider it to be the most beautiful of all white variegated plants. The striped canes reach about 2 m (6 ft) and are clothed with drooping leaves 30 cm (1 ft) long which have a broad white margin. They eventually become tatty lower down and should be cut down each or every other winter to encourage new shoots. Although it grows quite well permanently out of doors in mild areas it is far better to grow it in a tub and take it in during the winter. A position in full sun and free-draining soil is best.

Planting for harmony and effect

All the large-leaved perennials listed in this book will take on a more exotic and unusual character when mixed and planted with the trees, shrubs and climbers described in this chapter. Wherever space permits, they should be planted in bold groups of a minimum of three or five for proper impact. Herbaceous plants, even large-leaved ones, should never be dotted about. Large clumps or groups convey the beauty and character of the plant far more fully, and it is better to have a smaller number of varieties where space is limited, than to reduce too much the size of the individual clumps. They will appear scaled-down anyway in some instances, especially when used as companions to large subjects such as palms and bamboos and even phormiums.

Ligularia dentata 'Desdemona' will, as here, produce purplish tints on top of its leaves if grown in the sun. In the shade they will be greener but bigger.

The number of options open when selecting plants for grouping together is immense, and so the suggestions I make here do not have to be firmly adhered to by any means: they are simply combinations which I know from experience work well. Remember, too, when planning a grouping that it is not just simply which plant looks good with another, but whether they are happy with the same types of conditions – sun, shade, moisture etc.

PLANTING WITH PALMS

The Chusan palm, *Trachycarpus fortunei*, rates first among my choice of desirable large plants and when small – up to 2 m (6 ft) – would be best encircled or underplanted with either the evergreen fern *Blechnum tabulare* or the deciduous ostrich fern, *Matteuccia struthiopteris*. Rodgersias such as *R. podophylla* or *R. tabularis* (or both) would look good, as would *Hosta sieboldiana elegans* and *Ligularia dentata* 'Desdemona'. All would benefit from the light shade that the palm fronds would supply.

THE BEAUTY OF BAMBOOS

Bamboos should be situated either close to water or so that they screen part of the view, creating mystery, or perhaps diverting a path. For this the taller *Phyllostachys* varieties would be best. They are most beautiful when they arch over water or can be planted both sides of a path to create a tunnel effect. As regards companions, they are very versatile and any of the large-leaved herbaceous plants look good when planted around them. When close to water they are particularly well matched when placed alongside clumps of gunnera. Bamboos make very attractive woodland plants as an underplanting for trees, providing they only receive light shade. The large-leaved *Sasa palmata* looks especially good in this

situation and could be grown with *Fatsia japonica* or any other of the woodland shrubs.

Phyllostachys nigra should be grown in an open sunny position such as in the middle of a lawn to retain the blackness of its stems, and the little golden-striped *Arundinaria viridistriata* must also have sun for good coloration. This, grouped with the golden-leaved *Hosta* 'Sum and Substance' and the golden cut-leaved elder *Sambucus racemosa* 'Plumosa Aurea' makes a lovely splash of sunshine.

PHOTOGENIC PHORMIUMS

Where there are palms there should always be bamboos and phormiums, their size merits them as the 'bones' of an exotic garden. The lovely purply-leaved *Phormium tenax purpureum* with *Hosta sieboldiana elegans* planted around its feet cannot be beaten for beauty of colour combination and architectural contrast. The creamy yellow-striped *Phormium tenax* 'Variegatum' would also prove spectacular planted with hostas with cream or yellow-edged leaves. Other good companions for phormiums are the acanthus and *Crambe cordifolia*. A group of all three would give a very distinctive and interesting picture both in leaf and flower, the white gypsophila-like flower heads of the crambe harmonizing with the white and purple flower spikes of the acanthus, and the great blackish purple flower spikes of the phormium. All require an open sunny situation and so would be happy together.

A TRULY EXOTIC COLLECTION

For those possessing a conservatory or greenhouse the following arrangement of tender plants would be a *pièce de résistance*. Such an assemblage would be the envy of neighbours and the height of exoticism.

The focus of this collection of treasures would be the majestic Abyssinian banana, *Ensete ventricosum*

(*Musa ensete*), with at its feet a ginger, *Hedychium gardnerianum*. The stunning combinations of *Melianthus major* with *Canna×generalis* 'Wyoming', and *Canna iridiflora ehrmanii* with *Ricinus communis* 'Gibsonii' should also be included. On the other side of the purple-leaved canna we should have the white variegated reed *Arundo donax* 'Variegata', and last but not least the sumptuous *Hibiscus moscheutos* 'Southern Belle'. On the perimeter of this group but still in full sun we should have a couple of hardier specimens: *Eucalyptus niphophila* and *Paulownia tomentosa*, and perhaps *Cordyline australis* underplanted with purple- and white-variegated pittosporums. Close by but lightly shaded, perhaps by a Japanese poplar, *Populus lasiocarpa*, could be the huge white pendulous-flowered *Datura cornigera* and the rice paper plant, *Tetrapanax papyriferus*.

SUB-TROPICAL SHADE

Deserving a dell of its own is the breathtaking tree fern, *Dicksonia antarctica*, perhaps sharing its privilege with the treasured *Rodgersia tabularis* with (for contrast) *R. podophylla*. Nearby could be a few more familiar shade-loving plants: *Fatsia japonica*, camellias, pieris, and those aristocratic hydrangeas, *H. aspera* and *H. sargentiana*, underplanted with that lovely partnership of *Hosta sieboldiana elegans* and *Ligularia dentata* 'Desdemona'.

These examples have brought together the best of both worlds in terms of hardy and non-hardy subjects. There are, of course, countless other possibilities, and the great fun is to experiment and to try alternatives until you reach an individual, personally satisfying result.

CHAPTER 6

Large-leaved perennials in containers

We generally think of flowers when planning plants for outdoor containers, but foliage can be equally effective, especially when bold and decorative.

The range of containers available now is probably greater than ever, all shapes and sizes, plain or fancy and in a number of different materials. Pots and containers especially when grouped together greatly enhance an area of paving or terrace, whatever the situation, and are much more effective than when scattered about individually.

Siting

A patio area is of course the first situation to come to mind when thinking of placing containers, but they can be placed virtually anywhere in the garden to good effect. Corners and edges of terrace or paved areas are more clearly defined when pots are placed on them. The areas around swimming pools or formal ponds are enhanced by groups of pots. If placed either side of doorways or steps they give definition, and add a decorative note if placed either side of garden benches. Very small gardens of only a few square metres are best paved and the plants confined to pots which can be alternated, and enclosed courtyards which are usually paved or gravelled are very appro-

Bold leaves of contrasting shape *and* texture: (LEFT) *Peltiphyllum peltatum* and (RIGHT) *Hosta sieboldiana elegans* by the waterside.

priate areas for them. A pot placed at the side of the start or the end of a path makes a note. In general containers, especially if planted with striking subjects, can do much to emphasize the design of the garden.

Which plants?

Some plants are actually happier in containers than in the open ground, enjoying the freer drainage which is provided, and can be given special soil if need be. They also obtain increased soil warmth which is beneficial to tender plants, which can then be moved under glass for the winter. Incidentally arum lilies (*Zantedeschia aethiopica*) if grown in pots and overwintered in the conservatory or greenhouse will begin flowering in midwinter.

Lilies and other bulbous plants often do better in pots where a suitable well-drained sandy soil or humus can be provided, and where they are less prone to damage by slugs or other bulb-eating pests. One bulbous family, *Eucomis*, is particularly attractive in a pot because this raises it to a higher level where it can be appreciated more easily, and the leaves, which would normally lie untidily on the ground, hang over the edge of the pot.

Naturally the pots and containers themselves make the plants more decorative but the smaller plants in particular benefit from being raised to a higher level. Take hostas, for example: the big-leaved varieties obviously look distinctive in pots, but it is the smaller

55

leaved ones which benefit most from closer inspection. Incidentally, hostas are certainly among the most attractive of foliage plants for containers, and they come in so many varieties of different size and leaf colour that there is one suitable for any pot.

Big-leaved perennial plants are not often chosen for pot culture, which is a pity as many, such as acanthus, ligularias and phormiums make very handsome pot plants. One of the greatest advantages of having plants in containers is that they can be moved around so that the groupings or their positions can be changed if we get bored, and it also enables us to move any tender plants into the conservatory or greenhouse for the winter.

Containers can be used to grow a plant which we like but which is too invasive to be planted out. Petasites, for example, is a wonderful foliage plant but not one which most of us would want to smother the whole garden. Grown in a pot and kept damp, its huge leaves can be enjoyed without fear of it taking over.

Other plants in containers

Container gardening is practised more widely than ever now, and it is probably the most practical form where very small gardens are concerned and is some-

Pots accentuate steps far better when planted with bold architectural plants such as arum lilies and purple cordylines.

times the only method available in some instances such as with roof gardens.

In these situations it is obviously still desirable to grow as *wide* a range of plants as possible to create sufficient interest.

There are many shrubs and even trees which can be grown in pots and tubs, which, added to the herbaceous plants (including of course some large-leaved perennials), and, if desirable, such things as bulbs, means that there is no reason why a container garden should be a dull one.

Trees and shrubs will naturally be restricted in growth and in some instances may benefit from pruning so their root systems can maintain their stem and leaf structure, but the most important thing to ensure is that they are watered and fed regularly to compensate for the root restriction.

If pots are grouped together it makes watering much easier and is certainly more practical if automatic irrigation systems are used. Other advantages are that some shade or protection may be given to some of the plants, and, as when house plants are grouped together they create a microclimate around themselves. The same guidelines for plant association and groupings which I have given for beds or borders can be used here, and as the plants are in pots can be easily changed around or experimented with if desirable.

It is just as important with containers as with the border to include some evergreen plants and shrubs, as a collection of empty pots in winter is just as gloomy as an empty border. Plants such as phormiums and bergenias, and shrubs like camellia, choisya and *Fatsia japonica*, and even some bamboos such as *Arundinaria murielae* are invaluable. Remember too that some plants are only semi-deciduous. In mild or average winters, plants such as acanthus and many ferns remain almost evergreen. There are even a few evergreen climbers such as *Clematis armandii* and ceanothus which could be grown on fan-shaped trellis panels in pots. The wide range of ivies, some of which are variegated, can also be useful. The larger forms are best used as climbers while the smaller varieties make very attractive trailing plants useful for softening the edges or sides of containers.

So, as we see, the scope for creating beauty and interest when using containers is quite large.

Arranging containers and plant care

When grouping pots of plants together we should follow the same rules as we would when using them in the border and consider contrast of shape, form, colour and, if possible, texture. One advantage over planting in a border is that differing soil requirements are no longer a problem, as each pot can be filled with a suitable mixture.

Using a phormium as a background subject in the biggest pot, for example, it could be fronted by an acanthus, a ligularia and finally a hosta. Here we have achieved variety of form, colour and texture. Continuity could be provided by planting them in pots of all the same design but of different sizes.

When considering containers for plants, the size of the plant will dictate the size of the container but allow for plants to increase in size and remember that the larger the container the less quickly it will dry out.

You will need to provide a good soil for your containers (garden soil will not do). A special tub and pot compost is available, but most plants also require or benefit from liquid feeding, usually once a fortnight. Give a top dressing of fresh soil once a year (removing the top few inches of the old soil and replacing with new) and where possible every four years or so

57

remove the plant from its container (in winter with deciduous plants and spring for evergreens), remove as much of the old soil from around the roots without damaging them and repot in fresh compost.

Which pot?

If a plant is very ornate or architectural in its leaf shape then it is more likely to be set off in a pot of relatively simple design, whereas a plant of simple shape might look better in a fancy pot, but these are not hard and fast rules and individual taste will obviously play an important part. It would be a pity, however, to destroy the beauty of a plant with a pot of too elaborate a design, therefore simpler designs are usually safer.

Cost obviously plays a part when choosing containers but other things must be taken into consideration. Weight, for example, can differ enormously, especially with the larger sizes. A 75 cm (30 in) diameter terracotta pot will probably require two people to lift it even empty, whereas the fibreglass look-alikes are only a fraction of the weight, and also a fraction of the price. Terracotta pots breathe and so will dry out more quickly than fibreglass or plastic and therefore suit plants liking free drainage. Moisture lovers are happier in plastic or other non-porous pots.

There are, however, some disadvantages. Small pots will dry out very quickly in summer and will need watering every day, so an automatic drip-feed watering system is something to consider if you are going away. Another disadvantage is that during severe weather the soil may freeze. Again, the small pots are most vulnerable, the larger ones may only freeze on the outside. This can be prevented to a certain degree by tying sacking round them.

In severe weather it may be advisable to group *all* your containers together. This way they will not only protect each other but it will be more practical and easier to give them some additional protection of straw or sacking. Another method is to bury the pots in the soil. Pots will also be given some protection if placed against the wall of the house, and this way will be even easier to give additional protection.

These problems are few, though, when compared to the pleasure we may get from growing plants this way. From the tiniest paved yard to the grandest of terraces or swimming pool areas, containers play an essential part in completing an attractive picture which can only be enhanced if our large-leaved perennials are added to the normal choice of flowering and other plants.

Large leaves may be solid or finely divided and contrast well together, as here with the hybrid *Lysichiton* and the royal fern *Osmunda regalis* with primulas in the foreground.

CHAPTER 7

The plants

DESCRIPTIONS WITH NOTES ON CULTIVATION

ACANTHUS (Acanthaceae) BEAR'S BREECHES

The combination of handsome leaves and beautiful flowers make the acanthus one of the best herbaceous foliage plants. Not surprisingly, its strong architectural leaf shape has been used from Greek and Roman times in decorating buildings, and this quality should be exploited when positioning this plant in the garden.

Acanthus mollis *Italy*

Long in cultivation, this plant has long, deeply lobed dull green leaves and the usual prickly flower spikes of pinky mauve and white about 90 cm (3 ft) tall, which are quite plentifully produced. More handsome is the variety *A. m. latifolius*, which has larger, arching leaves 90 cm (3 ft) long of deep dark glossy green, but the flowers are not so freely produced.

Acanthus spinosus *S. Europe*

The dark green leaves, 60–90 cm (2–3 ft) long, are deeply divided and have spiny points. This is probably the most free-flowering. *A. spinosissimus* has even more finely cut and prickly leaves but, like other available species, *A. balcanicus* and *A. perringii*, is less garden worthy.

Bold large-leaved perennials grouped in pots show contrast of form, shape and texture:
1. **Phormium tenax**
2. **Ligularia dentata 'Desdemona'**
3. **Acanthus mollis 'Latifolius'**
4. **Hosta sieboldiana elegans.**

Acanthus are happiest in full sun where they will flower in any good but fairly well-drained soil. Best planted when young, they do not move well when established, sending down long tap roots which inevitably break off in the process.

A. m. latifolius is probably the best of the bunch. Though not over generous with flowers it is certainly the most handsome in leaf. Flower arrangers should use gloves when cutting the flowers which have hard very prickly calyxes.

AMICIA (Leguminosae)

Amicia zygomeris *Mexico*

A very individual looking tender handsome foliage plant, with strong stems to over 2 m (7 ft) carrying large tri-lobed leaves. The large yellow flowers with maroon markings are a tell-tale indication of its family. It likes good soil and plenty of sun but will only succeed in sheltered gardens in mild areas.

ARALIA (Araliaceae)

Aralia cachemirica *Kashmir*

Huge rosettes of rich green and much divided leaves topped in summer with a panicle of ivory flowers (which are followed by maroon-black berries), give this plant a very lush, almost tropical appearance. At nearly 2 m (6 ft), this plant should be given a prominent position such as on the curve or the centre of a border. It would make a beautiful focus point by a pond or

waterfall where the climate does not permit a tree fern (*Dicksonia antarctica*).

Aralia racemosa   N. America

Of slightly smaller stature than the previous aralia, and of more upright habit, this carries greenish white flower heads on dark stems. Though graceful it does not possess the lushness of *A. cachemirica*.

These species will grow in sun or dappled shade in any good soil. They die down to the ground in winter whereas the other kinds, though mostly deciduous, retain their stems.

ARISAEMA   (Araceae)

Arisaema speciosum   Himalayas

I have only included this one species as the others are of rather small stature and this has probably the best leaves: three-lobed, bright green with maroonish edges supported on mottled brown stems standing about 60 cm (2 ft) high. The flowers, or correctly spathes, which are the main attraction of these plants are, in this species, deep purplish maroon inside, striped with the same outside on short stalks so that they are held beneath the leaves. The ivory spadix has a thin purplish extension 50 cm (20 in) long giving the plant a very strange appearance. Arisaemas require a sheltered position preferring humusy soil and dappled shade.

Ligularia wilsoniana. This is one of the largest leaved ligularias and also one of the tallest in flower, often producing its yellows spires 2.5 m (8 ft) in length.

ARUNCUS (Rosaceae) GOAT'S BEARD

Aruncus dioicus *Northern Hemisphere*

Often listed under the synonym *A. sylvester*, this huge ferny plant is like a giant astilbe. The thick mound of bright green leaves 1.2 m (4 ft) high is overtopped in summer by a further 60 cm (2 ft) of great plumes of ivory coloured flowers making it a great feature plant, especially for the waterside. The finely divided leaves are a splendid contrast to the huge solid ones of gunneras and lysichitons and their fresh green colouring a lovely foil for the purple-leaved *Ligularia dentata* 'Desdemona' or *Rheum palmatum tanguticum*.

It tolerates most conditions but is happiest in good moist soil, sun or dappled shade and is easily propagated by division.

ASPIDISTRA (Liliaceae)

Aspidistra lurida *China*

This tender but tough evergreen plant will be familiar as a houseplant. The broad dark green leaves are hardly beautiful but its stemless maroon flowers are a curiosity. It likes shade in any good soil.

BEGONIA (Begoniaceae)

Begonia evansiana *Japan, China, Malaysia*

Yes, a hardy begonia, and the only one. It is every bit as attractive as its tender companions. The glistening waxy leaves have pinky red-tinged undersides, and stems and the flower buds of the same hue open to sprays of pale pink. It reproduces by little bulbils and, though modest in height at 45 cm (18 in), is worthy of any garden in a warm spot in sun or dappled shade. There are white and large-flowered forms.

BERGENIA (Saxifragaceae) ELEPHANT'S EARS

Bergenia ciliata *Nepal, Kashmir*

By far the most beautiful in leaf of all the bergenias, the huge round leaves, 30 cm (1 ft) across, are very hairy on both sides and quite different from the other leathery leaved bergenias. They are, however, frost-tender, making it a deciduous species, whereas the others are evergreen. The stems are hardy and soon push up large heads 30 cm (1 ft) high of pale shell pink flowers in spring.

B. ciliata makes stunning underplanting for the tree fern (*Dicksonia antarctica*), appreciating the dappled shade of its crown of fronds, but is too beautiful and unusual to use as ground cover under ordinary shrubs or for the edges of borders or beds, for which the other kinds are more suited. It seems to thrive particularly well when grown on a slope.

Bergenia cordifolia 'Purpurea' Siberia

Vastly superior to the ordinary form, the greatest asset of *B. cordifolia* 'Purpurea' is that its bold round leaves take on purplish tints in winter. The tall strong stems of magenta flowers in spring make this one of the tallest of the tribe, in the 60 cm (2 ft) region.

HYBRIDS

'Ballawley'

An excellent plant in foliage and flower. Less stiff oval leaves 30 cm (1 ft) long, shining green are topped by sprays of crimson flowers 60 cm (2 ft) high. Though not so colourful in winter it is one of the best for summer display but should be given a little shelter and dappled shade to do its best.

'Silberlicht'

One of the few white-flowered varieties with handsome leaves make this a useful alternative to the usual purple-flowered kinds. The snowy white flowers, around 30 cm (1 ft) tall, turn pale pink with age.

'Sunningdale'

A feature of this plant is the coral red flower stalks supporting vibrant carmine flower heads. The foliage assumes rich winter colouring. Growing about 30 cm (1 ft), it is considered by some to be the best yet available.

The richest winter coloration of the foliage is achieved in positions exposed to sun and wind and often poorish soil which makes them valuable plants for difficult positions. Their greatest asset, however, must be their value in softening the hard lines of paving and brickwork and for accentuating the curves of beds or borders where their spreading rhizomes form carpets of excellent groundcover foliage. The clumps are easy to divide for propagation.

BESCHORNERIA   (Amaryllidaceae)

Beschorneria yuccoides   Mexico

This extraordinary plant has always reminded me of those wonderful rain-forest plants, the bromeliads but, as we see, it belongs to the amaryllis family. A large tuft of slightly flaccid sword-like blue-grey-green leaves 60 cm (2 ft) high after a few years throws up an enormous arching flower spike 2.5 m (8 ft) long, consisting of coral pink bracts from which dangle apple green bells, a breathtaking sight.

It needs to be thoroughly 'baked' to flower well and by far the best position would be on a sunny rockery or in paving. I have seen a dramatic example planted high up on a rock face. A most exotic-looking plant, but unfortunately only suitable for warm gardens.

BUPHTHALMUM   (Compositae)

Buphthalmum speciosum   S.E. Europe

A rather coarse plant with paddle-shaped leaves and large deep yellow daisies which last for several weeks. It is useful for rough ground where it will spread rapidly to form ground cover and rise to 1.5 m (5 ft) level. I much prefer the similar looking but less invasive *Inula magnifica*, which is even larger.

CALTHA   (Ranunculaceae)
GIANT MARSH MARIGOLD

Caltha polypetala   Caucasus

For bog or shallow water. Tall succulent stems 60 cm (2 ft) high carry the almost water-lily-like veined leaves and the buttercup flowers. Intriguingly, legend has it that this plant was originally stolen from the Vatican gardens, though I cannot imagine why. However, it is most suited to the margins of large ponds or lakes, where it spreads by long runners.

CANNA   (Cannaceae)

Canna indica   S. America, W. Indies

The so-called Indian shot, with coppery-green leaves and small reddish flowers is the least exciting of these tender plants. It reaches 1.2 m (4 ft).

Canna iridiflora ehrmanii   Peru

A choice and desirable plant, and possibly the hardiest, thriving in warm gardens in our climate. The huge banana-like blue-green leaves, 90 cm (3 ft) long, are overtopped by elegant arching spikes of beautiful small rich rose pink flowers, making the whole plant often as much as 2.5 m (8 ft) high. It is one of the most exotic-looking things we can grow here and as such one of the best for creating a tropical effect. It survives

**Rockwork by a small pond with (LEFT) *Peltiphyllum peltatum*
and (RIGHT) *Rodgersia podophylla* which, growing in a sunny
position, has taken on purplish tints.**

67

**Lagoon with backcloth of *Lysichiton americanum* (LEFT) and
Gunnera manicata.**

in the warmest gardens if given a good mulch at the end of the autumn, but is best lifted and potted up, and placed in a frost-free conservatory or greenhouse until late the following spring. This way it will shoot forth and flower by midsummer. It is stunning when placed alongside purple-leaved subjects such as the annual *Ricinus communis* 'Gibsonii' or the shrub *Cotinus* 'Grace'.

HYBRIDS

'Malawiensis'
A very striking variety, the leaves having narrow stripes of lemon yellow and the usual large gladiolus-like flowers, a bronzy orange.

'Le Roi Humbert'
A feature of the famous Red Border at Hidcote, Gloucestershire, England. Its foliage is a rich purple with a faint green feathering, and the flowers are like bright red gladioli, around 1.8 m (6 ft).

'Wyoming'
The best of the purple-leaved kinds, though not the most vigorous, with broad leaves of a deep rich purple. The flowers in apricot orange clash a trifle for my taste but the foliage makes the most beautiful possible foil to *Melianthus major*. Like all cannas it should be grown in full sun in rich moist soil.

Cannas have been used as summer bedding for formal plantings in public parks since Victorian times and are still commonly seen today. But their beauty is marred when used this way in straight rows or blocks.

Although their roots are not frost hardy they are as tough as old boots and need no more attention than dahlia tubers. Lift them in late autumn, store them in a dry frost-free place until early spring, then divide and pot up and start them into growth at about 15°C (60°F) and harden off before planting out in late spring.

CARDIOCRINUM   (Liliaceae)

Cardiocrinum giganteum   *W. China*

A real showstopper if ever there was one, growing 1.8–3 m (6–10 ft). Thick stems taper from a basal rosette of huge arum-like leaves above which long greenish white trumpets with maroon throats 20 cm (8 in) long hang down from the visible stem. It was once remarked on as being 'like a woman whose great beauty is marred by her having thick ankles!' It needs deep leaf mould in woodland and the bulbs (which should be planted with their noses just below the surface) should be planted in groups of different ages to achieve annual flowering, because they take about seven years to flower. An expensive practice, but if you can afford it, and can supply the conditions this plant requires then you will be well rewarded.

CAUTLEYA   (Zingiberaceae)

Cautleya spicata   *Himalayas*

One of the few hardy gingers, not as exotic-looking as its tender relatives, but none the less a very attractive subject when grown in a bold group. The stems of opposite rows of long green blades are topped with maroon bracts with deep yellow flowers about 60 cm (2 ft) high, perhaps taller in very rich soil.

Sun or dappled shade suit best and as a precaution a good mulch in winter. This should be grown at the front of the border and is particularly nice when grown with a group of *Lilium candidum* whose flowers of similar coloration accentuate those of the cautleya.

CLEMATIS   (Ranunculaceae)

Clematis × heracleifolia   *China*

There is always doubt on first sight of this plant as to its correct labelling. A herbaceous clematis? Yes, indeed.

Not a spectacular plant but one whose foliage seems to draw attention, which is why I have included it.

The large divided leaves have wiry stems and taller leafy stems bear little blue scented flowers 90 cm (3 ft) high, which are followed by fluffy silvery seed heads. Any soil in sun will do. Attractive with hostas.

CRAMBE   (Cruciferae)

Crambe cordifolia   Caucasus

Even if the huge mound of rather coarse puckered heart-shaped leaves are not to everyone's taste, the great sprays of tiny white, scented gypsophila-like flowers usually are. At 2 m (6 ft) high and nearly as much across, they are a great sight especially when swarming with butterflies. It will not (infuriatingly) succeed in rich moist soil, insisting on poor and well-drained earth in which it sends down its long tap roots. It prefers full sun. The very brittle roots can be divided for propagation as long as each piece has a crown.

CURTONUS   (Iridaceae)

Curtonus paniculatus   S. Africa

Looking like a giant crocosmia, this individually striking plant has broad ridged blades 90 cm (3 ft) long and arching sprays of fiery orange trumpets topping 1.2 m (4 ft). Like crocosmia it prefers full sun and is not fussy as to soil. The foliage almost merits it as a subject for 'exotic' plantings but the flowers are not quite up to scratch for that purpose. Propagation by division.

DRACUNCULUS   (Araceae)   DRAGON PLANT

Dracunculus vulgaris   Mediterranean

I include this plant as a novelty more than for any other reason, though it does possess rather large coarse divided leaves on 60 cm (2 ft) spotted stems. But undoubtedly its main feature, albeit a monstrous one, is the enormous crimson spathe 45 cm (18 in) high with its maroon-black spadix. To top it all it smells most foully of rotting flesh. The large tubers should be planted 15 cm (6 in) deep in well-drained soil in full sun. It suits pot culture well. Of similar curiosity are the smaller and less offensive arisaemas.

EREMURUS   (Liliaceae)   FOXTAIL LILY

Eremurus robustus   Turkestan

All the foxtail lilies, of which this is the largest, are very similar in appearance, differing only in colour and size. The untidy long limp strap-like leaves lay on the ground and have begun to wither by the time the flower spikes develop. The pale pink, small starry flowers of E. robustus are massed on a spike 3 m (10 ft) tall and shaped like a giant lupin. They are best set off with a dark background. The huge star-fish shaped roots, which are very brittle, should be buried just beneath the ground in well-drained soil in full sun. They leave a hole when they die back and are therefore best placed at the back of the border. There are other smaller species in other shades and some splendid hybrids, notably 'Shelford' and 'Highdown', some of rich colouring.

EUCOMIS   (Liliaceae)

Eucomis pole-evansii   Transvaal

Very rare in cultivation, this strikingly unusual bulbous plant is only suitable for the warmest gardens. From long glossy 15 cm (6 in) wide leaves arises a stout central stem 1.5 m (5 ft) high with a huge pineapple-shaped flower head consisting of a mass of tiny star-shaped flowers topped with a tuft of leaves 25 cm (10 in) across like a pineapple – an unforgettable sight.

It is probably best grown in pots (in full sun) and would make a decorative patio subject and grown this way it benefits from the additional soil warmth in summer and could be moved under cover in extreme weather in winter. There are smaller more easily obtainable kinds: *E. bicolor*, which is one most frequently met with, and *E. punctata*. The unusual and exotic character of these plants deems them appropriate subjects for the 'exotic' garden (see Chapter 5).

FILIPENDULA (Rosaceae) MEADOW SWEET

Filipendula camtschatica (syn. gigantea) Kamchatka

Lording it over all the other waterside plants with exception of the gunnera, the 3 m (10 ft) straight stems clothed with jagged palmate leaves are crowned with large flat frothy flower heads of either ivory or pale pink, 30 cm (1 ft) across. A truly grand plant, ideal for mixing with other noble plants for bog and waterside. Dappled shade and acid soil is where it is at home.

Filipendula rubra E. United States

The queen of the prairies, though of lesser stature than *F. camtschatica* at around 2 m (6 ft), is none the less dramatic in that it forms very substantial leafy clumps of the same palmate leaves, and has generous flat heads of pink flowers, best in the form 'Venusta'. This form is more vigorous than *F. camtschatica* but would make a superb waterside plant in any large garden.

A stream-lined planting showing a variety of strong leaf forms: (TOP) *Peltiphyllum peltatum*, (BOTTOM LEFT) *Lysichiton americanum*, and (RIGHT) *Rheum palmatum*.

The coloration of its flowers renders it a lovely companion to both purple-leaved ligularias, white arum lilies and the blue-grey-leaved hostas such as *H. sieboldiana elegans*. The smaller *F. purpurea* has flowers of a vibrant cerise, a bit overpowering for most gardens. All these plants prefer very moist, even boggy conditions in good soil and dappled shade.

GLAUCIDIUM   (Glaucidiaceae)

Glaucidium palmatum   *Japan*

Something of a treasure but requiring cool acid soil in woodland. The delicate pale mauve poppy-like flowers 60 cm (2 ft) tall are held above big lobed fresh green leaves.

GUNNERA   (Haloragidaceae)

Gunnera manicata   *S. Brazil*

'Lovely big rhubarb' was the last comment I overheard of this plant, and quite descriptive at that. The first experience of meeting this plant is always memorable, even to non-gardeners.

In spring from huge creeping rhizomes, the leaves push skyward, great prickly stems with their folded umbrellas to ultimately rise and expand to 2 m (6 ft) or more high and the same across, deeply lobed and as rough as sandpaper. The flowers consist of huge cones 1 m (3 ft) high of rusty brown when their seed is ripe. In all a plant of unparalleled drama, requiring a position by water or in marshy ground. It reaches its ultimate size if well fed and grown in light shade, though it is quite happy in full sun. The crowns should be covered in winter first with bracken and then by the plant's dead leaves which should be turned upside down and folded on top of it.

Gunnera scabra (syn. *chilensis, tinctoria*)

Of smaller stature having smaller leaves (to 1.5 m (5 ft) across), more puckered and serrated, on shorter stalks. The flowers remain for some weeks after the leaves have died down, a strange sight!

HEDYCHIUM   (Zingiberaceae)   GINGER LILY

These noble plants with their banana-like leaves and almost orchid-like blooms are truly exotic and as such best fitting in association with others of similar character – bananas, palms, bamboos, cordylines, cannas, phormiums and the like (see Chapter 5). They are only suitable for very mild gardens; although their roots will survive colder areas they do not make sufficient growth to flower, coming up too late in the season. They like a rich moist soil in full sun and their roots, which are thick fleshy rhizomes, should be planted just beneath the surface. In winter when the stems die down they should be covered with a thick mulch. Propagation is by division.

Hedychium coccineum   *India, Burma*

The strong stems carry opposite pairs of narrow fleshy leaves terminating in flower spikes with coral red petals and red stamens 90–120 cm (3–4 ft) high. The variety 'Tara' which originated from Wakehurst seems a trifle hardier.

Hedychium densiflorum   *E. Himalayas*

In this species the 90 cm (3 ft) spikes have rich orange petals and coral red stamens. The best variety is 'Assam Orange' of slightly larger proportions.

Hedychium forrestii

This is the hardiest of the bunch, and makes lush and leafy clumps over 2 m (7 ft) high. The flower spikes, though smaller and less dramatic than the others, are a change in that they have white petals with projecting orange stamens.

Hedychium gardnerianum   N. India

This is the most majestic of the race, bearing huge stems clothed with broad blue-green blades 38 cm (15 in) long. The 25 cm (10 in) flower spikes have long yellow petals and orange-red projecting stamens. In rich soil in a warm spot this plant will attain 1.8 m (6 ft). If it is grown in a tub in a frost-free greenhouse for the winter it will remain evergreen and flower earlier as a result the following year. Stunning when planted at the foot of the great Abyssinian banana (*Ensete ventricosum*).

Hedychium greenii   Bhutan

The distinctive foliage is dark blue-green and at only 60 cm (2 ft) adds interesting variety to the race.

Hedychium × raffillii

This is a hybrid between *H. gardnerianum* and *H. coccineum*, and a fine plant. The 1.5 m (5 ft) stems with broad leaves have brilliant orange petals and dark red stamens, finer than *H. coccineum* but not as hardy.

HERACLEUM   (Umbelliferae)   GIANT HOGWEED

Heracleum mantegazzianum   Caucasus

An exciting plant but one with a notorious reputation. Like a giant cow parsley towering 3 m (10 ft), sometimes 4 m (12 ft) in the air, its great cartwheels of tiny white flowers on stems like huge sticks of celery make a magnificent show in woodland or rough places. But it is not suitable for the average garden in that it seeds invasively and the large leaves, 1 m (3 ft) across and much divided, die back early, leaving a huge hole. One can control it by removing the flower heads before they set seed. Heracleums give a wonderfully exotic effect, especially when grown with other statuesque plants. The notorious reputation I mentioned earlier is due to the fact that if roughly handled in strong sunshine it can cause blistering and sometimes a most unpleasant purple staining of the skin. I once saw an old church graveyard which had become entirely engulfed in a forest of heracleum, making it rather reminiscent of *The Day of the Triffids*!

HOSTA   (Liliaceae)   PLANTAIN LILY

As mentioned in Chapter 1, there is such a huge number of varieties of these first-class popular plants available now, that they have their own volume in this series, so I shall just describe briefly those which have particularly large leaves.

Hostas are one of the best plants for ground cover, growing in sun or shade but usually preferring dappled shade in good moist soil where their leaves will be largest. They are a splendid contrast to sword-shaped leaves, grasses and ferns and are lovely in association with waterside plants. The leaves of many of them remain in pristine condition throughout the season but the glaucous-leaved kinds should be placed away from the drip of trees. They are very prone to slug and snail damage and poison should be spread when the leaf spikes appear. Most have spikes of lilac coloured flowers but the foliage is the main beauty of these plants.

Hosta crispula   Japan

Large dark green leaves with wavy edges, broadly margined white. One of the best and most striking of the white-variegated kinds when well grown. It is more beautiful when grown in shade, and reaches around 75 cm ($2\frac{1}{2}$ ft).

Zantedeschia aethiopica 'Crowborough'. The familiar arum
lily will succeed if heavily mulched in winter.

An unusual use of *Hosta sieboldiana elegans* entirely
fringing a small lagoon.

Hosta fortunei 'Albo-picta'   *Japan*

At its most beautiful in spring when the leaves are bright yellow with dark green margins. These colours eventually tone down to two soft shades of green in summer. 75 cm (2½ ft).

Hosta fortunei 'Marginata Alba'

Less striking than *H. crispula* but of softer beauty, with sage green corrugated leaves with bold white margins. 75 cm (2½ ft), happiest in shade.

Hosta fortunei 'Obscura Marginata'

Broad leaves, this time with a creamy yellow margin (which gave it its old name 'Yellow Edge') which is retained through the season. 75 cm (2½ ft).

Hosta 'Fringe Benefit'

An American introduction with large puckered leaves with a broad white margin. Happy in sun or shade. 90 cm (3 ft).

Hosta 'Honeybells'

A descendant of *H. plantaginea* but of lesser stature. The pale lilac flowers have inherited the perfume of its parent but the leaves have more undulating margins. A first-class plant, staying in good fetter well into the autumn. 75 cm (2½ ft).

Hosta 'Krossa Regal'

Large, glaucous green arching leaves with undulating margins. Forms a lush and impressive clump at 90 cm (3 ft).

Hosta plantaginea   *China*

A rare and noble plant with large, arching glossy bright green leaves. In autumn it produces large white beautifully scented trumpet flowers. This plant requires a warm sheltered spot in dappled shade to succeed. 75 cm (2½ ft).

Hosta 'Royal Standard'

Similar to but a little smaller than *H. plantaginea*, one of its parents. 90 cm (3 ft).

Hosta sieboldiana   *Japan*

Very large broad grey-green leaves to 40 cm (16 in) form a lush mound, the flowers barely rising above the leaves.

Hosta sieboldiana elegans

The most sumptuous of hostas and infinitely superior to the ordinary form, with almost round blue-grey, strongly ribbed and puckered leaves 30 cm (1 ft) wide, forming huge striking clumps. It is stunning with purple-leaved plants such as *Ligularia dentata* 'Desdemona' and is happiest in dappled shade 90 cm (3 ft).

Hosta sieboldiana 'Frances Williams'

In effect, a gold-edged *H. s. elegans*. In good clones the margins are of an almost mustard yellow; in poor sorts they are more beige. A first-class and desirable plant, whose foliage remains in pristine condition well into the autumn. 75 cm (2½ ft).

Hosta 'Snowden'

Large pointed sage-green leaves form a mound sometimes 90 cm (3 ft) in height, overtopped by a further 30 cm (1 ft) of strong spikes of white green-tinged flowers. One of the most impressive of all hostas both in leaf and flower. Best in dappled shade.

Hosta 'Sum and Substance'

The leaves, which are reminiscent of *H. sieboldiana*, start green but mature to a beautiful golden yellow, making it the largest in leaf and one of the most spectacular of all yellow-leaved hostas. It will grow in sun or shade but is probably best in light shade where the leaves will be partly greeny gold. The usual lilac flowers rather clash.

Hosta ventricosa   E. Asia

An impressive plant, the shiny handsome dark green leaves being strongly veined and heart-shaped, with undulating margins. The flowers are of much richer colouring than is usual among hostas. 1.2 m (4 ft).

Hosta ventricosa 'Variegata'

The *ventricosa* leaves are here boldly margined with deep cream, making it a very striking plant. It is not as vigorous as some and should be encouraged by feeding and watering.

INULA   (Compositae)

Inula magnifica

A stately plant magnificent for the bog garden or waterside. Huge paddle-shaped 1.2 m (4 ft) long leaves form basal clumps above which strong stems rise to 2.5 m (8 ft), forming branched heads of deep yellow daisies 12 cm (5 in) across. *I. racemosa* is a larger but coarser plant only suitable for rough wild places. Happiest in sun, these plants will tolerate dry conditions but prefer soil where their deep tap roots can reach moisture. Easily propagated by division.

KIRENGESHOMA   (Saxifragaceae)   *Japan*

A much over-rated plant. The leaves, which remind me of those of the plane tree on dark wiry stems, are topped in late summer with sprays of pale yellow flowers at the 90 cm (3 ft) level. It prefers dappled shade and moisture.

LIGULARIA   (Compositae)

A distinctive race of plants which we should not be without where water is present. They prefer rich damp or boggy soil, where they soon form very substantial clumps which benefit from division every few years. They are best grown in dappled or light shade as full sun often wilts their leaves. They are much loved by slugs and snails so precautions will need to be taken early in the season as growth starts.

Ligularia dentata 'Desdemona'   China

Probably the most popular of all the ligularias, the striking leaves dark green on top while their undersides and stems are a rich dark reddish purple. In sun the tops of the leaves are often tinged the same. The branched daisy heads, at 1.2 m (4 ft) tall are a rich orange. This is a beautiful companion to *Hosta sieboldiana elegans* and makes a stunning contrast to white variegated bog irises.

Ligularia 'Gregynog Gold'

A noble plant of grand proportions, bearing large round leaves with toothed margins and great conical spikes of vivid orange flowers 1.8 m (6 ft) high.

Ligularia macrophylla   Orient

A desirable and rare plant quite different from all the other ligularias, having large grey-green horseradish-like leaves 75 cm (2½ ft) long with prominent central white ribs. The dense short spikes of yellow flowers are most handsome at around 1.5 m (5 ft).

77

Variety of form with (FROM LEFT) *Miscanthus, Osmunda regalis* **and** *Hosta sieboldiana* **by the water.**

A tropical glade featuring the Abyssinian banana *Ensete ventricosum* as a centrepiece.

Ligularia × palmatiloba

A hybrid between *L. dentata* and *L. japonica* and a great improvement on both, having handsome broad leaves with deeply toothed margins and candelabra spikes of orange daisies 1.2 m (4 ft) high.

Ligularia przewalskii   *N. China*

The triangular, deeply incised, dark green leaves have wiry black stems and flower spikes 1.8 m (6 ft) high carrying narrow spines of small yellow daisies. 'The Rocket' is the best form and *L. stenocephala* is a similar but less striking plant of lesser stature. These plants must have shade even in boggy soil as the leaves flag with the least bit of sun, giving the plant a very untidy appearance.

Ligularia veitchiana   *China*

Large, slightly triangular, heavily veined leaves 30 cm (1 ft) across are borne on stout triangular stems and the 1.5 m (5 ft) high columnar flower spikes consist of small yellow daisies.

Ligularia wilsoniana   *China*

Similar to *L. veitchiana* but when established becomes a larger and more handsome plant. The slightly smoother leaves stand 90 cm (3 ft) high on hollow triangular stems and the flower spikes, clothed for 90 cm (3 ft) of their length can reach 2.5 m (8 ft) high. Dappled shade will prevent the huge leaves from collapsing and a good rich soil should be provided. The flowers are followed by fluffy seed heads. One of the most dramatic plants for the waterside.

LYSICHITON   (Araceae)   SKUNK CABBAGE

Along with the gunneras these are among the most architectural plants for the waterside, bog garden or streamside. They have to be planted in the young state as they strongly object to being moved once established, sending down their great tap roots 90 cm (3 ft) or more. Their huge leaves damage easily and they should be placed out of strong winds in a hollow or where they would be protected by other plants. They should be planted in very rich soil in which plenty of manure has been incorporated and fed annually.

Lysichiton americanum   *N. America*

In spring just as the leaves are emerging the large striking yellow spathes with their green spadixes appear, 30 cm (1 ft) high. The rosette of huge shiny paddle-shaped leaves when the plant is mature can reach 1.2 m (4 ft) and makes a handsome companion to gunneras. The leaves retain their beauty until the autumn.

Lysichiton camtschatcensis   *Kamchatka*

The whole plant is of somewhat smaller proportions than *L. americanum* but the flowers are snowy white and the leaves a beautiful pale glaucous green. In gardens where both have been growing for a number of years a hybrid (still unnamed) has arisen. This supersedes both in vigour, resulting in a plant often reaching 1.8 m (6 ft) in height. The 45 cm (18 in) tall spathes are a beautiful cream with green spadixes and the leaves a lovely pale glaucous pea-green, obviously inherited from *L. camtschatcensis*. A spectacularly beautiful and dramatic plant which always draws attention and admiration.

MACLEAYA   (Papaveraceae)   PLUME POPPY

Macleaya microcarpa   *China*

An impressive foliage plant forming bold clumps of 2.1 m (7 ft) felty white stems clothed with fig-shaped grey-green leaves white underneath. The whole is topped with branched plumes of flesh or coppery-buff fluffy flowers. 'Coral Plume' is a variety of richer coloration and *M. cordata* has white flowers.

These plants make a lovely tall accent among lower growing species. They are said to do best in sun but I have known them to luxuriate in shade. However, they do prefer reasonably well-drained soil. Propagation is simple in that it runs quite freely at the root.

MELIANTHUS (Melianthaceae)

Melianthus major   *S. Africa*

A plant needing no introduction to foliage lovers and undoubtedly one of the most beautiful. The gracefully poised stems are clothed with divided deeply serrated leaves, the whole of a lovely grey-green. In mild areas the plant produces its flowers with dark maroon bracts and green stamens in autumn or winter, but these are of no great beauty and by this time the plant is usually losing its lower leaves. Although it does best in warm gardens (as it is tender) where it will remain evergreen, it is far better to cut the stems down each winter, when it will shoot vigorously in the spring to form a bushier, more compact plant. The coloration of this plant makes it a stunning companion to purple foliage, such as *Cotinus coggygria* 'Royal Purple' but especially the tender *Canna×generalis* 'Wyoming'. It should be grown in full sun and protected with a thick mulch of forest bark in winter.

MUSA (Musaceae) BANANA

Musa basjoo   *Japan*

The only banana which will survive our winters, and then only in the very warmest parts. The slender trunk is topped with the huge paddle-shaped blue-green papery leaves which unfortunately tear in the wind. At 3 m (10 ft), it is undoubtedly impressive especially when grown (which indeed it should be) with other exotic-looking things such as palms, bamboos, cordylines and phormiums. This plant should be placed in the most sheltered position possible but in sun and in rich moist soil. It will greatly benefit from regular feeding and watering and often flowers as a result. As with most bananas when this happens the plant begins to die but produces several offsets or side shoots. It should be well wrapped up with bracken or straw in winter but if the winter is severe, and it is cut to the ground it may still shoot forth from the ground again in summer.

MYOSOTIDIUM (Boraginaceae)

CHATHAM ISLAND FORGET-ME-NOT

Myosotidium hortensia   *Chatham Islands*
A distinct and highly individual-looking plant and one to be treasured. The leaves, reminiscent of *Hosta sieboldiana elegans*, are rich green and glossy, 25 cm (10 in) across and long. The sprays of tiny flowers are forget-me-not blue. It is a notoriously difficult plant, only thriving in warm gardens and even so it must be covered with cloches for the winter. The secret in less favourable gardens is to grow it as a pot plant, feeding it regularly with seaweed fertilizer and keeping it in a frost-free greenhouse or conservatory for the winter. A worthwhile effort. It is usually grown from seed.

PELTIPHYLLUM (Saxifragaceae)

UMBRELLA PLANT

Peltiphyllum peltatum
This plant has recently been re-named *Darmera peltata*, but is still generally listed by nurseries and reference books under *Peltiphyllum*.

81

Hosta sieboldiana elegans, **one of the largest and possibly
the most splendid of all hostas.**

Melianthus major, possibly the finest foliage plant, here displaying its maroon flowers. It should always be accompanied where possible by *Canna×generalis* 'Wyoming'.

Sometimes called the poor man's gunnera, this is a first-class big or waterside plant, forming wonderful lush clumps of its bog round scalloped leaves each 38 cm (15 in) across. The whole plant often standing 1.5 m (5 ft) high. The thick snaky rhizomes are a strange sight, especially in spring when they send up long bristly flower stalks topped with heads of almost bergenia-like flowers. These are almost over before the leaves appear.

It likes a rich peaty moist or boggy soil at the water's edge where its rhizomes will form a colony. Though it is happy in sun it grows taller in the shade and is easy to multiply by lifting sections of the rhizomes with a spade, ensuring that each has a growing point. This is an indispensable plant for any collection of waterside plants and would be a good substitute for a gunnera where there is not sufficient space for one of these giants.

PETASITES (Compositae)

Along with the big polygonums, these are among the most invasive of plants, making them unsuitable candidates for all but the largest gardens. They make ideal ground cover, smothering everything in their path and they will grow particularly well in heavy wet clay in shade where little else will flourish and so are valuable for that purpose.

Petasites hybridus *Britain*

The native British butterbur can be seen on long stretches of river banks, the huge kidney-shaped leaves 90 cm (3 ft) across often stand 1.2 m (4 ft) high and are glaucous with ivory veins and serrated margins.

Petasites japonicus giganteus *Japan*

More refined than the previous species, of the same proportions but with fresher green leaves of cleaner shape. If you have a rough patch of bog or stream in woodland or a shady bank of a lake then this will add beauty and variety if added to the other waterside giants, gunneras, lysichitums and peltiphyllums, soon forming a huge colony.

The flowers of both these species, which appear in early spring before the leaves, consist of rosettes of pale mauve or white flowers sitting on the ground, a curious sight and popular with flower arrangers.

PHORMIUM (Liliaceae) NEW ZEALAND FLAX

Among the most architectural of herbaceous plants, valuable as evergreens but especially for creating a sub-tropical effect. The most colourful forms are unfortunately the most tender and even the plain green form, *P. tenax*, can be killed in severe winters. The base of the plant is most vulnerable and should be surrounded with a thick mulch of forest bark in winter and the leaves tied up to prevent snow damage. They like full sun and shelter from strong winds and a good moist soil. The flowers, which overtop the leaves by a good margin, are reminiscent of *Strelitzia reginae* (bird of paradise flower), but of dark dull coloration, none the less very dramatic and architectural. They are easy to propagate by separating one of the fans of leaves, ensuring it has some root, and potting in well-drained sandy soil in as small a pot as will contain it, retaining it under glass until established.

Phormium cookianum *New Zealand*

Suitable for the most sheltered gardens only. This and its varieties differ from the *P. tenax* forms in that they are of more modest height, 90–120 cm (3–4 ft) and have more lax leaves. The best variety is 'Tricolor', which is striped red, yellow and green. The flowers are brownish with reddish filaments but are less often produced than on the bigger *P. tenax* forms.

Phormium tenax   *New Zealand*

In mild, sheltered gardens the leaves alone can reach 3 m (9–10 ft), while the dark blue flowers, which have a whitish bloom, will overtop them by a further 1 m (3 ft) or so. The form 'Goliath' is a vigorous clone with wider leaf blades.

Phormium tenax purpureum

In this the leaves are of a reddish purple hue but this varies greatly, some plants being almost green and so a good colour form should be sought. 'Dark Delight' is the richest and darkest of the purple forms but is a hybrid between *P. tenax* and *P. cookianum* and so has shorter, more lax leaves. 'Purple Giant' is the largest, with bronze-purple foliage.

***Phormium tenax* 'Variegatum'**

A much over-used plant but none the less attractive for its boldly cream and yellow striped leaves which give more of a contrast to the dark red flowers covered in a white bloom. Because of their very tough consistency the flowers remain a decorative feature many months after they have finished. There is a more beautiful yellow-variegated form called 'Williamsii', whose leaf blades contain more yellow than green but it is sure to be more tender. Crosses between *P. tenax* and *P. cookianum* have resulted in a number of very colourful variegated offspring in shades of salmon pink, orange, red and yellow.

PHYTOLACCA   (Phytolaccaceae)   POKEWEED

These large, lush, leafy plants make a bold accent in the border and have an individual though slightly coarse character. They do best in sun or light shade and should be underplanted with ground cover such as bergenias to complement them. They develop huge thick rhizomes and should not be moved when large.

These plants seed quite readily and are fast-growing; they appear to live to a considerable age. The whole plant is poisonous.

Phytolacca americana   *Florida*

In this species candelabra-like stems terminate in small spikes of white flowers which are followed by dark maroon berries.

Phytolacca clavigera   *China*

More attractive than *P. americana*, in that the flower spikes are pink, and in autumn the stems turn bright crimson, constrasting with the yellow leaves and jet black berries.

POLYGONUM   (Polygonaceae)   KNOTWEED

I have included these largely on account of the size of their leaves; although *P. cuspidatum* 'Spectabile' is undoubtedly beautiful, they are all disastrously invasive and should be confined to little islands in large lakes.

***Polygonum cuspidatum* 'Spectabile'**   *Japan*

It is easy to be lured by the beauty of this plant, whose 2.5 m (8 ft) succulent stems, pinky red in spring, are clothed with eye-catching alternate large heart-shaped leaves marbled cream, butter-yellow and green. It is less invasive than the plain green kinds but will still run amuck causing havoc in a small garden. It must have dappled shade or the leaves will scorch.

Polygonum sachalinense   *Sakhalin Islands*

The worst culprit, forming forests of 3.5 m (12 ft) high canes almost like bamboo, and sending underground runners several metres or yards at a time. The male plant has attractive small vertical ivory white fluffy flower spikes between the huge green heart-shaped leaves, which are each 25 cm (10 in) long.

85

Ensete ventricosum (syn. *Musa ensete*), the Abyssinian banana, is a giant but tender perennial which can be grown from seed.

Hedychium gardnerianum, a member of the ginger family, is
best pot grown and overwintered under glass to guarantee
flowers the following year.

RHEUM   (Polygonaceae)   ORNAMENTAL RHUBARB

A bold, highly decorative plant, both in leaf and in flower, especially beautiful when planted by the waterside, and a possible substitute for a gunnera where space does not allow. They like a rich, moist but not boggy soil in sun or dappled shade and if space permits should be planted in threes to produce a really lush effect. They should always be included with rodgersias, ligularias and the like for contrast and variety of leaf shape. They are best propagated by removing the side crowns (which they freely produce) in winter or early spring. (The common rhubarb is *R. officinale*.) Most flower in late spring.

Rheum australe (syn. emodi)   *Himalayas*

A rare species with huge entire heart-shaped leaves with red veins and undulating margins. The erect flower spikes, over 2 m (7 ft) high may be white or red.

Rheum palmatum   *China*

The most frequently seen, with large, deeply cut and serrated leaves standing 1.8 m (6 ft) high, topped by crimson flower spikes.

Rheum palmatum 'Atrosanguineum'

In this form of the above, the leaf buds and emerging leaves are bright red and the leaves retain a reddish coloration underneath when mature. The flower spikes are great fluffy panicles in cherry red.

Rheum palmatum tanguticum

The best form, producing new leaves further into the season which are purple tinted on top when young as well as retaining colour underneath, and with less deeply serrated margins. The flower spikes, though less vivid, are most handsome – usually ivory (contrasting well with the purple) or sometimes pink.

Beautiful when planted with a margin of silver lamium (*Lamium maculatum* 'Beacon Silver').

RODGERSIA   (Saxifragaceae)

Indispensable plants for the waterside, especially streams and ponds where their splendid, characterful leaves and beautiful astilbe-like flowers add invaluable variety to the other noble and architectural subjects. They like moist or marshy ground in sun or dappled shade, especially thriving in acid soil rich in leaf mould. They spread fairly freely and are easily propagated from the creeping rhizomes.

Rodgersia aesculifolia   *China*

The leaves are like those of a horse-chestnut, bronzy five-lobed but about 45 cm (18 in) across. The branched flower spikes can be ivory or pale pink.

Rodgersia pinnata   *China*

Leaves are similar to the above, but arranged in pairs; the flowers are soft pink. Well known is *R. p.* 'Superba', one of the best, with very bronzy leaves and bright, slightly salmon pink flowers on dark stalks. A stunning contrast to *Hosta sieboldiana elegans*.

Rodgersia podophylla   *Japan*

Big, distinctive star-shaped leaves with jagged edges sometimes 60 cm (2 ft) across. They are bronze when young and if grown in a sunny position take on purplish tints in summer. The rather sparsely produced flowers are creamy ivory. A good contrast to *R. tabularis*.

Rodgersia sambucifolia   *China*

Less often seen, but a very handsome plant with distinctive pinnate leaves gracefully poised, and elegant sprays of creamy white flowers.

Rodgersia tabularis *China*

The choicest of the race and much sought after. It is said that the huge circular pale green, scalloped leaves can reach 90 cm (3 ft) across, but they are more usually 60 cm (2 ft). The small ivory flowers are held well above the leaves, 1.5 m (5 ft) high. *R. tabularis* must have dappled shade or the leaves will scorch. A plant to be treasured and a lovely companion to *R. podophylla*, *Ligularia dentata* 'Desdemona' or the fern *Matteuccia struthiopteris*. This plant is sometimes called *Astilboides tabularis*, incomprehensibly as it bears no resemblance to an astilbe whatsoever.

RUMEX (Polygonaceae)   WATER DOCK

Rumex hydrolapathum *Britain*

A rather coarse but handsome plant with great spear-shaped leaves of some architectural quality. However, this plant's greatest value lies in the russet colour of the flower heads produced in late summer and the crimson autumn coloration of the foliage. It should be grown in shallow water, preferably on the margins where its foliage can give contrast to other waterside subjects.

SENECIO (Compositae)

Senecio smithii *S. Chile*

Another subject for shallow water but of more handsome appearance, with thick dark green, spear-shaped leaves and branched heads of white, yellow-eyed daisies 1.2 m (4 ft) high. These are followed by fluffy seed heads. Can also be grown in a damp border but is happiest with its feet in water. Propagation is by division.

SILPHIUM (Compositae)   PRAIRIE DOCK

Silphium terebinthinaceum *N. America*

The weedy daisy-like flowers let down what is otherwise a noble plant. The mound of long-stalked, big dark green leaves 90 cm (3 ft) high is topped by a further 60 cm (2 ft) of flower stems, which I would cut off as they destroy the beauty of the plant's handsome leaves. It likes sun and any good soil.

SMILACINA (Liliaceae)   FALSE SPIKENARD

Smilacina racemosa *N. America*

Like some exotic solomon's seal, a deservedly popular plant. Dense clumps of arching stems terminate in creamy ivory fluffy flower spikes, like small astilbes but beautifully scented. It likes shade and acid humusy soil, preferably with plenty of leaf mould. It can be divided for propagation but it is a shame to spoil large established clumps.

TRACHYSTEMON (Boraginaceae)

Trachystemon orientale *Caucasus*

This plant's greatest quality must be that it will grow in dry shade. A good ground cover plant with large rough rounded leaves the size of *Hosta sieboldiana*. It must be sheltered from wind or its leaves will bruise each other. The strong rhizomes spread quickly along the ground. Lovely electric blue flowers appear in early spring just as the leaves begin.

VERATRUM (Liliaceae)

Noble plants prized for their beautiful pleated foliage. They take a number of years to mature and should be planted when young as they resent movement when established. They require deep rich moist soil and

Myosotidium hortensia, the Chatham Island forget-me-not,
is a much prized plant – tender but thrives if fed on seaweed.

Beschorneria yuccoides, exotic and dramatic, but somewhat
tender, has to be baked to flower well.

shade to prevent scorching of their splendid foliage. They mix well with most bold foliaged plants but are especially attractive when grown with groups of turk's cap lilies.

Veratrum album   Europe, Siberia

The leaves of all species are very similar being large – 30 cm (1 ft) – long, oval and pointed, and heavily pleated, encircling strong stems. The flowers are the easiest means of identification; those of *V. album* are greenish white in a dense narrow spike up to 1.8 m (6 ft) high.

Veratrum nigrum   Europe, Siberia

The most striking in flower, with spikes of maroonish black 1.8 m (6 ft) high. Large clumps make a stately and dramatic sight and are much to be treasured. If space were limited then this should be the choice, but otherwise all three listed here are first-class plants.

Veratrum viride   N. America

Nature displaying her great colour harmony in an all-green plant, flowers and all. This has possibly the best and largest leaves but is usually of lesser stature than the two above, reaching about 1.2 m (4 ft) but occasionally more.

VERBASCUM   (Scrophulariaceae)   MULLEIN

Verbascum vernale   unknown

The huge rosettes of silvery white furry leaves are of sufficient beauty in themselves and are complemented by the 1.8 m (6 ft) tall stately spikes of vivid yellow flowers. Like all furry leaved plants it abhors wet, liking a well-drained soil. To keep the splendid leaves in mint condition it is best grown in gravel and as a foreground subject in full sun. It seeds quite readily.

YUCCA   (Liliaceae)   PALM LILY

These plants are barely herbaceous but since we have included phormiums which are similar, architecturally speaking, it seems only fair to include the best species, which certainly qualify as large-leaved. I should warn the unwary, however, that most possess stiff and viciously pointed leaves making them totally unsuitable candidates for gardens with children, and adults should beware, too! All the species are exotic in effect but only of great beauty when in flower as the foliage on its own, with the possible exception of *Y. recurvifolia*, is rather dull. All require full sun and free-draining soil, and freely produce side shoots which can be separated, potted and rooted under glass.

Yucca filamentosa   S.E. United States

The usual rosette of stiff grey-green leaves 90 cm (3 ft) across is well cleared by the equally stiff flower spike which bears lustrous creamy bells, beautifully fragrant, 1.5 m (5 ft) high.

Yucca flaccida   S.E. United States

With narrower leaves than *Y. filamentosa*, and less dangerous, being limp and having drooping tips. The flowers, which have longer side branches, are generously produced.

Yucca gloriosa   S.E. United States

The most frequently met with of the species and one of the largest. The stiff rosette of leaves is topped by flower stems often 2.5 m (8 ft) high but they often appear so late in the season that they become damaged by frost.

Yucca recurvifolia   S.E. United States

Foliage-wise a splendid plant. Probably the best and most magnificent of the species, it combines the qualities of laxer, longer leaves and more elegantly poised flower spikes rising 2.5 m (8 ft) high. Happily, these are produced enough in the season to avoid frost.

ZANTEDESCHIA (Araceae) ARUM LILY

Zantedeschia aethiopica S. Africa

The well-known lily of the Nile, a handsome plant both in foliage and flower, is unfortunately disliked by some due to its decorative use at funerals. When in flower, clumps or drifts of them by streams or ponds, with their big white sails lit up by the glossy dark green leaves, are a wonderful sight. It should always be included in waterside plantings; though succeeding in the border it does seem to prefer to have its feet in the mud. Can also be grown in water providing the crowns are at least 15 cm (6 in) below the water (and frost) level. The form 'Crowborough' is said to be hardier but I often wonder if there is any difference. For the collector there is a beautiful green-throated form called 'Green Goddess', which has larger glaucous green leaves. It beats *Z. aethiopica* in height, often reaching 1.5 m (5 ft) and is certainly hardier. I am sure it is popular with flower arrangers.

Zantedeschias should be grown in rich soil for good flowering and their crowns protected with a thick mulch in winter. If grown in pots in a frost-free conservatory or greenhouse they will flower in midwinter.

Dicksonia antarctica, the hardiest of the tree ferns, may be
grown permanently out of doors in the mildest gardens.

Index

Page number in *italics* indicate illustrations

95

ACKNOWLEDGEMENTS

The publishers are grateful to the following for granting permission to reproduce the colour photographs: Myles Challis (pp. 2/3, 15, 79, 82, 86, 90 & 91); Michael Nicholson (pp. 19, 22, 27, 87, & 94); David Crampton (p. 42); and Garden Picture Library (p. 83). All the remaining photographs were taken by Bob Challinor.

The publishers are also grateful to the John Lewis Partnership for granting permission to undertake photography at the Longstock Water Garden and also to Mr J. Bond for granting permission to undertake photography at the Savill Garden, Windsor Great Park. All the line drawings were drawn by Rosemary Wise.